TAKING ACTION

The practical guide to making an impact

Roy McCloughry

frameworks

For Joanna, Elizabeth and Lauren
with love.

FRAMEWORKS
38 De Montfort Street,
Leicester LE1 7GP, England

© The Kingdom Trust 1990

Unless otherwise stated, Scripture quotations in this publication are from the Holy Bible, New International Version. Copyright © 1973, 1978, 1984 International Bible Society. Published by Hodder and Stoughton.

First published 1990

British Library Cataloguing in Publication Data
McCloughry, Roy
Taking action: the practical guide to making an impact.
1. Great Britain. Pressure Groups
I. Title
322.4'3'0941
ISBN 0-85111-209-9

Set in Palatino
Typeset in Great Britain by Spectrum Graphics
Printed in Great Britain by Richard Clay Ltd,
Bungay, Suffolk

Frameworks is an imprint of Inter-Varsity Press, the book-publishing division of the Universities and Colleges Christian Fellowship.

CONTENTS

ACKNOWLEDGMENTS

Many people have been very encouraging about this project and I would like to thank them all for their help. They are too many to name. I would like to mention my wife Helen who did a lot of the research for the book and who read it several times in draft, making it a much better book than it would otherwise have been. Charles Sherlock from St John's, Nottingham also read the book and helped to put it into the Australian context. Francis Bridger was also of great help on the issues surrounding local politics. Readers will soon notice that the book is written mainly for the British and the Australian contexts though I hope that it will be helpful to a much wider readership.

I would also like to thank those churches who support me in my ministry through the Kingdom Trust. The ministers and congregations of All Souls, Langham Place, London, St Paul's and St George's, Edinburgh, St Peter's, Farnborough and St Nicholas', Nottingham have given me tremendous backing and encouragement. This book is for them. It is their book in many respects and I hope that in some small way it will enable them to make an impact on the society in which God has called them to live.

Taking action is the companion to another book entitled The eye of the needle (IVP, 1990), which looks more deeply at the tensions involved in living as a Christian in the modern world.

Finally, many thanks to Simon for agreeing to write the foreword to a book which will probably be the cause of a lot more work for him!

FOREWORD

When I heard that the remains of Shakespeare's historic Rose Theatre had been discovered at the bottom of a building site in my London constituency, I was naturally delighted. But when I realized that this was to be all but destroyed by the concrete foundations of a new building I, with many others, was stirred to action. Eventually, after much campaigning and media coverage, and even though we were not completely successful, the campaign managed to force the owners to save a much larger part of this unique element of our national heritage. The experience was a powerful reminder to me of how important it is to know the way that effective protest works.

As a Member of Parliament I am always encouraging people to participate in the local, national and global community in which we live. For too long now many people, and I include committed Christians here, have refused to face up to many of the challenges of living in the real world. They have not wanted, or been able, to handle the obstacles which must be overcome if significant changes are to be brought about. This is why I warmly welcome this new 'how to' book from my friend Roy McCloughry.

Taking action is a really useful practical guide on how to involve oneself in influencing some of the decisions that are made around us every day of our lives. Its use of examples, checklists and guidelines shows informed insight and authenticity. The book will give many people the principles, the practice and the encouragement with which they can go out to make the best impact in the society in which they live.

Simon Hughes, MP
House of Commons

What will people say about us at our funeral? We'd all love to know. Will they be struggling for words or will our lives present them with an em-barrassment of riches from which to choose? And who will be there? Will it be a service attended by family and a few friends? Or will people

LIFE: VOCATION OR VACATION?

crowd in to the church to pay tribute to some-one whose life touched theirs in a very special way? What will be the tone of the service? Will a note of praise and thanks to God sound with a sureness above the grief?

Wouldn't we all like to know? But ask your-self now, how many people are grateful to God for all you've done for them, for the way you've served them and fought for their rights?

Your life can make a difference. You have one life to live and God has given it to you to use in his service. What can you do to ensure that you will?

Look at the state of the world. Look at the loneliness and the misery. God wants to use you to meet need, to reach out in love, to burn for justice. God wants you, yes you, to get your hands dirty.

(Matthew 25: 35-40)

Let's not be like the Chinese proverb which says, 'Of all the thirty-six alternatives, running away is best.'

Some people don't want to take action because of the commitment involved. While it may be true that some ways of being effective may be time consuming, the beauty of acting together is that we often have only a small (but important) part to play.

"Wouldn't we all like to know?"

You can be effective as part of a larger effort with very little time commitment. Take Amnesty International as a good example. They are involved in the struggle to uphold human rights across the world, and campaign to free prisoners of conscience. When we phoned them up and asked how they enabled an individual to take action, they said that the main thing was writing letters!

Every couple of months they send supporters a list of six prisoners and a sample of an appropriate letter and the individual is asked to write and protest to the government concerned. No marching in the street, no great expense, just a few letters. Yet you are involved.

"...running away is best."

Life is not a vacation to be squandered on ourselves. It is a vocation, a calling to make our lives count in the service of others.

*e*ndless possibilities

Just think of the possibilities! They're like a mouth-watering menu with so much choice that the waiter is hovering over your table, ready to take your order, and you're saying, 'I'm afraid I'll need a few more minutes.'

The fact is that when you decide to take action, the problems of the world turn into a series of challenges. Rather than moaning about pollution you can actually join an organization like Friends of the Earth or ARK and report instances of pollution to them, knowing that they will take action. Instead of merely talking about the needs of the disabled you can help in a holiday-home for the disabled.

It may seem at first that the endless possibilities are contrasted with your finite abilities and you may feel depressed by this. But this is in fact the key to sorting out your calling. Instead of this being a turn-off, think of it in this way: *'How can I match the possibilities with my abilities?'* In other words, what are you already interested in that you could use? Most people have some skill, hobby, interest or work experience which somebody else is crying out for.

Don't start thinking about scaling mountains before you can climb hills! Start by taking action in areas which are familiar to you and then move on as you gain confidence.

"So relax...!"

Also, before you start you will imagine all sorts of problems. But the problems you imagine before you start are often not the ones you encounter when you take action. They are more practical – about how to get things done – than the great philosophical problems you imagined beforehand. So relax – you might even enjoy yourself!

*M*aking a difference

So many people get 'het up' about the state of the world and then shrug their shoulders as if to relieve themselves of any responsibility.

They imagine that only powerful people who are 'already in the know' influence the decisions which matter in our society. But you can influence the quality of education at your local school, join a housing action group, keep a watching brief on planning applications in your local area which might threaten the quality of life in the community, or lobby your local councillor over environmental-health issues.

If you feel that 'personal service to others', rather than social and political action, is more your style, you can help others with voluntary work, or visiting the homebound or bedridden and doing chores for them. This could be either visiting an elderly person and listening to their stories and showing you care or becoming a 'buddy' to somebody living with AIDS who is too weak to do much for themselves.

The fantastic thing is that *you can make a difference to the lives of others*! You don't have to be educated or rich or beautiful. You just have to be motivated enough to get some information and then take action. As you're reading this book you're already on the right tracks.

"...becoming a 'buddy' to somebody living with AIDS ..."

(See 1 Corinthians 1:27-31)

*b*eating the clock

You may feel that you have no time to get involved with something else, but this may not be as true as you think. I don't want to seem unsympathetic to you but how much time do you spend each week watching television?

Now add on the number of hours in your week which are 'dead time'. That is time which you could free-up for something else if you tightened up a little. Be honest with yourself. Everyone has dead time in their week.

The fact is that although we say that we watch television to 'relax', an evening in front of the box can be very tiring. I can almost guarantee that if you gave up one 'telly' evening and spent those hours getting involved effectively in a project you would benefit a great deal from it yourself.

You may, for example, be a busy student who has only one hour a week, but you could visit somebody regularly for that hour or you could write letters for some campaign. And, although this book is not primarily aimed at students, even one hour a week used consistently can be of great help.

*O*vercoming fear

O.K., you admit that you've got some time. But you are still holding back. The problem is quite natural. It's called fear. You see yourself as launching out into 'the great unknown' and are more than a little reticent. Maybe you've suddenly realized that the course you've chosen will mean going to meetings and there will be *people* there. And you know that you're painfully shy. Or you are sure that when you visit your first new disabled friend with cerebral palsy, you will not be able to understand anything he says because he has a speech impediment.

"These are real fears..."

These are real fears. Don't keep them to yourself. Share them with others. If you are a Christian, pray honestly about them. If you can, have a bit of laugh at yourself in the presence of God. Then remember this: everyone who takes action feels inadequate at first, but *focus on the needs of others rather than on your own inadequacies, and your fears will diminish*. Remember that 'perfect love casts out fear'. When you are engaged in loving others you become less self-conscious.

(1 John 4:18)

Take comfort from the fact that in taking action you are being obedient to the great command to 'love your neighbour as yourself'.

(Matthew 2:39)

r eady, steady, go ...

One of the keys to effective action is preparation. Information is a good thing. It shows you where you fit in to the larger picture, answers common questions which you may have been asking and may help to show you that your fears are groundless. Good information will nearly always show you that there is more that you can do than you thought.

Why don't you do what we did when we compiled 'The user-friendly guide to taking action', which appears at the back of this book? We thought of some issues which might make good illustrations of how people could take action. We then asked around for names of groups in those areas and phoned them up. Sometimes friends helped with names, other times the local library was a help or the local church minister. Even the yellow pages were helpful, or an appendix at the back of a relevant book with a list of related organizations.

One book, the *Voluntary Agencies Directory* published by the National Council for Voluntary Agencies, contains over two thousand organizations that would value some help. (Try your local library.)

So why be a moaner on the sidelines? If you can breathe, think, talk, write and use your hands, you can make a difference.

"...where you fit in to the larger picture..."

'i wouldn't know where to start.'

'You wouldn't catch me marching down the street with a banner, I'd be too embarrassed.'

'What's the point, the government will do what they like what ever I say.'

'Pray? There's no time to pray. What we need is some action!'

TALKING TACTICS

'Surely Christians shouldn't complain. Aren't we supposed to just put up with the bad things in life?'

'Why do we always have to talk about changing things? Isn't there anything good in our world we want to defend?'

Many people have a picture of those who 'take action'. They *would* march up and down the street waving placards and shouting slogans. They *do* talk passionately about politics all the time. They're certainly not the sort of person who would quietly enjoy soap operas at home on the telly.

*N*onsense!

These are just convenient stereotypes, the first line of defence we put up. We say, 'This is what such people are like'...'I'm not like them ... therefore I'm not cut out to be the kind of person who takes action.'

"I wouldn't know where to start."

Jesus said, '...*let your light shine before men, that they may see your good deeds and praise your Father in heaven*'. He assumes that we will want to do good to people in such a way that others, seeing our actions, are turned to God. There's no such thing as private Christianity. We are told to follow Jesus right out into the open.

(Matthew 5:16)

'O.K.', someone may say, 'I agree that as a follower of Jesus, I can't hide my light under a bushel (whatever a bushel is), *but taking action is not my style.*'

Before jumping to conclusions, let's look at the action menu. The first thing we find is that there are several action 'styles' to choose from.

*C*ampaigning – rocking the boat

Perhaps this is the one we all fear most, so we might as well tackle it first. For many people it arouses pictures of aggression and confrontation. It is associated with marching, public rallies, militancy and the gathering of petitions. We know because 'we've seen it on the telly'.

Perhaps there are two reasons why we are apprehensive about this.

"...marching, public rallies, militancy..."

Firstly, some of us don't feel *strongly* enough about anything to be able to stand in the pouring rain or collect signatures. We prefer to 'keep ourselves to ourselves' and our motto is 'don't rock the boat'.

Secondly, campaigning implies that we are up against an opposition whose views or actions we are attempting to defeat. Here the

"Passion and conviction..."

problem is that we don't feel *sure* enough about anything to back up our views with action. A lingering doubt may remain that they have a point and so we shouldn't challenge them.

Both of these are very reasonable fears. Passion and conviction often come only *as you begin to take action*. Armchair theorists can generate a lot of hot air about words but only activists get passionate about real people. So if you identify with these two fears, don't put the book down ... read on!

In my dictionary, campaigning is defined as 'a series of co-ordinated activities, such as public speaking or demonstrating, designed to achieve a social, political or commercial goal'.

This is very helpful. It shows us three simple things about campaigning which are important to remember.

Campaigning is:
- co-ordinated
- designed
- goal-orientated

Working together. It's very seldom the activity for one individual working alone, though history does contain examples of people who have lived and died for a single cause. The great campaigns such as the abolition of the slave trade or women's suffrage were co-ordinated efforts. Don't go alone. Find out who is bringing pressure to bear on the issue you have chosen and work with them. Good campaigning is well organized campaigning.

Effective campaigning has a design, strategy or plan behind it. It has a sense of timing which may come from much hard research and quiet diplomacy. Where you may have as much insight as a bull in a china shop, a good strategist knows when to apply the pressure and how. If a campaign is not planned strategically it will

"...when to apply the pressure and how."

fail, however sincere the campaigners might be.

A good campaign has clear goals. It may not be appropriate to work for the laws prohibiting abortion if the climate of opinion is hostile. But it may be possible to amend an existing act. If so, the goals set out must be capable of being achieved. In many campaigns people are beating their head against a brick wall because they do not have clearly defined goals which are attainable.

Another problem is that campaigners may have a good idea of what they are *against* but they may not have an equally clear idea of what they stand *for*. If you haven't got a very good answer, you could feel just a little foolish.

It's worth remembering, however, that we all have a 'right to be heard'. If you have a grievance or an idea for legislation don't be put off. Follow it through. Approach your Member of Parliament or elected representative. Try and get him or her on your side. If there is a professional group or body interested, try to get their support as well. This is what participation in society is all about.

Ian Greer, a professional and respected political lobbyist, gives the following advice, '... *keep on looking for support. When an idea gets sufficient support it becomes an issue. And if the issue is important enough it will eventually attract the attention, and the support, of those who can bring it into the national spotlight and eventually before Parliament.*'

"...you could feel a little foolish."

Ian Greer, *Right to be heard* (IGA, 1975), p. 21.

𝒫 ersuading – enter the debate

In our pluralistic democracy of many different viewpoints, the power of persuasion cannot be overstated. We do not believe in changing our society through violence. It is through people 'changing their minds' that a new climate of opinion is born in our country. In taking action this is of vital importance.

In his letter to the Romans, Paul talks about the 'transformed mind'. He says, *Do not be conformed to this world but be transformed by the renewing of your mind.* In other words, Christians are only distinctive in their actions because they are distinctive in their thinking. If we passively accept everything that the media and the advertising industry are throwing at us we will act (or not act) in the same way as everybody else.

(Romans 12:2)

The power of persuasion. Words do matter. Jesus said that the Holy Spirit would lead the disciples into 'all truth'. Our job is to persuade others of the truth that we believe in. This means that we must first attempt to show people where their assumptions and arguments are inadequate, weak, misguided or wrong and then effectively explain the truth as we perceive it. Our goal is not to defeat them by any means. It is to win them over by persuading them of the truth of our case.

"...words do matter."

As a result two kinds of people are unsuited to this task. There are those whose methods rather than objectives are not Christ-like. They may win the intellectual argument but if they don't treat people with respect and genuine love they will actually lose the person. I remember a brilliant American professor of theology debating with a humanist in public. He certainly won the intellectual argument. In fact he decimated her. But his attitude was cruel and unkind. He lost his audience who sympathized with her, and rightly so.

There are also some who put their own beliefs above the truth of Scripture. They feel at liberty to discard whole areas of Christian belief because 'modern' people cannot believe them. Christians should always face the difficulties thrown up by their faith, but we also have a prior commitment to the authority of Scripture as well as its relevance. When relevance becomes an absolute, all kinds of belief are negotiated away to make it easier to believe. For some, 'tolerance' even of things contrary to Scripture may become more important than truth. Nobody who believes that everybody is *really* a Christian is going to get excited about evangelism!

(2 Timothy 3:16)

*t*he three 'p's of persuasion

There are three stages in taking action by persuading. The first stage is to isolate the *problem*. People the world over will often agree at this level that there are massive problems in our world, whether they are in the area of green issues, nuclear war, child abuse, racism or something else. For example, one part of the problem of world hunger is that there is an uneven distribution of wealth between different nations.

The second stage is to derive from Scripture the *perspectives* to tackle the problems. This is the time for a little study of some good books on the issue concerned, or for listening to a few tapes by somebody who has some expertise in the area. Primarily though, it is time to soak yourself in the Scriptures themselves. If you need some help about the approach, I have listed some key books in 'The user-friendly guide' to help you.

The third and final stage in taking action is to ask: 'What do these perspectives tell us about our *practice*?' In other words, 'How should we then live?'

Here we must attempt to live out our beliefs or we will be lacking in integrity. It would be

"...face the difficulties thrown up by faith."

very unconvincing to push for greater overseas aid by our government and then be noticed for our own over conspicuous consumption and lifestyle.

Only those of us who can coherently stand up for what we believe and apply this to the actual world around us, are *really* taking action. Peter in one of his letters says, '*Always be prepared to give an answer to everyone who asks you to give the reason for the hope that you have. But do this with gentleness and respect, keeping a clear conscience, so that those who speak maliciously against your good behaviour in Christ may be ashamed of their slander.*'

(1 Peter 3:15-16)

Peter understands that part of the cost of standing up for what we believe in may well be that we are talked about behind our backs. As we seek to persuade people of the authority and relevance of the Christian message in the modern world we must live lives which measure up to our message.

*C*aring – reaching out in love

Some people who are uneasy about taking social action are more at home when they are caring for individuals. Both are expressions of our social concern. One person may campaign for pensioners' rights while another may visit the lonely in their homes or do the shopping for the housebound.

"...part of the cost of standing up..."

They can learn from each other. The campaigner may talk the language of justice and be tempted to get involved in the campaign but may neglect to love the elderly. The 'caring' visitor may get lost in the relationships she or he has with elderly people and neglect the fact that the condition of some of them is due to an injustice.

So the *campaigner* needs to be wary of drifting away from loving relationships, while the *carer* needs to be alert to the demands of justice. Loving relationships are not a substitute for justice.

Crossing boundaries of exclusion to love people rejected or ignored by our communities can be very costly and painful on a personal level. But it gives the love of God a high profile in a way that being involved in two-way loving relationships cannot do. If we associate only with those who are like us and are our natural friends we do not need the love of God for that. It is when we love those who are unlike us that we are closest to loving with the love of God.

So caring for people in a lonely fragmented world is not a second rate option. Love is the greatest thing in the world and expressing that love sacrificially is the greatest calling in the world. Pain, loneliness and frustration are often felt by those who act in unglamorous ways to help the poor and oppressed. They act because they care. It may not grab the headlines but it changes lives.

*a*cting – do it yourself!

By 'acting' I mean taking 'direct action'. We are all citizens and are called to be responsible in some way for the communities we live in.

My example here is the way dogs are allowed to dirty our streets. Don't laugh. I know there are many more serious subjects. But as one local councillor recently said to me, 'There's votes in dog dirt.' Apparently in the UK we complain frequently and volubly about the dirt on the streets. In this case, you could campaign for stiffer fines, or try to persuade dog owners of the need for dog hygiene. Or you could take direct action. Out you go with your 'poop scoop' and clean up the street yourself.

"...pensioners' rights..."

(1 Corinthians 13:5, 13)

"Love is the greatest..."

19

Immediately you do this you are in the middle of a political debate. Shouldn't the dog owners be doing this? Why should you be forced to do it? Aren't you making the problems worse by letting others off the hook?

Perhaps a different example might help. At a local nursery the paint is peeling off the walls and there is a general air of 'tattiness'. Why not get the parents in to do the place up? 'Because', say the teachers, 'it is the job of the education department to do it.' Why should we cover up their mistakes? It's a real problem.

"...the paint is peeling off the walls..."

But there are many situations in which direct action is very clearly the best way. Even if someone else has a statutory responsibility to act, you know that if you don't do *something* then nothing will be done.

Many people who feel that words and arguments are not their forte find that 'direct action' is their best route into taking action. There are certainly many opportunities to do something.

*p*rotesting – don't put up with it!

Our attitude towards declining standards is often one of acceptance. Yet Jesus calls us to do something about the situation. We are meant to be salt and light in the world.

(Matthew 5:13-16)

Salt was rubbed into meat to stop decay. Light shone in the darkness. If standards are falling or, to use Jesus' picture, the meat is going off, the question is where is the salt? We Christians are meant not only to be *in* society but *effective in* society. If the world is getting morally darker, where is the light of Christian protest and example?

"...where is the salt?"

*d*efending – credit where credit is due

Despite the many problems we see around us,

there is much that is good in the world which needs to be defended. Defending those things which are good is not the same as defending the *status quo*. Many people put up with the shortcomings of a situation because they don't want to 'bite the hand that feeds them'. They have grown rich in society as it is and therefore see little that is wrong with it. This blanket endorsement of life will not do.

Christians are called to be *discerning*. We are meant to be able to tell good from bad and right from wrong. We are neither to be so revolutionary that we want to overthrow everything, nor so conservative that we want everything to remain as it is. The Bible subscribes neither to naive optimism or to dark pessimism, but to an informed but radical realism.

There are many valuable approaches to taking action. Campaigning, persuading, caring, acting, protesting and defending. There's something for everybody on the 'action menu'.

"...something for everybody..."

*P*rayer is action too!

Praying isn't a separate activity, an alternative for those who don't want to get involved at all. Nor is it an optional extra. All the approaches I've mentioned are to be done prayerfully.

That is one of the things which marks out Christian social action. Paul says, '*...pray in the Spirit on all occasions with all kinds of prayers and requests. With this in mind be alert...*'.

(Ephesians 6:18)

Christians are different because they believe that prayer is effective. A person who doesn't believe in God is hardly likely to pray (except, perhaps, in an emergency).

Prayer shows several things. After all, we do not manipulate God through prayer.

• God is relevant to everything we do and works with Christians to bring about his plans

TAKING ACTION

for his world. He is always willing to listen to us however small the problem that we face.

• Prayer demonstrates faith in God. The only person we offend if we do not pray is God. (Prayerlessness in a Christian's life can be a tell-tale sign of unbelief.) Through prayer we show that we want to do his will.

• Prayer changes the world, both the people who pray and the people and situations which are prayed for.

These are startling claims. If you are not a Christian you might have thought that prayer was some kind of Christian cuddle blanket. Some see it as being nothing more than booing the umpire to make him change his mind. Christians, however, see it as a powerful demonstration of solidarity with God and his priorities. Our straightforward assertion is that prayer changes the world.

(Ephesians 6:10-18)

(1 Timothy 2:1-2)

"Prayer changes the world."

go for it!

You'll never know what you can do until you try. Ever heard that before? Agree with it? Why not try it!

There are literally millions of people in need of help from you. You can do something. Your life can make a difference. Put your faith into action, your mind into gear and go for it!

WORKBENCH

Check out your action plan

Time may be your biggest problem. 'I would like to do something but I'm so busy,' is a frequent response to the call to take action. Use the following checklist to sort out one or two priorities.

Q1. *How much time do you have a week for taking on a new commitment? Is the time in the evenings/weekends, or during the day?*

Q2. *Are you more interested in social and political action or in personal work?*

Q3. *Are you more focused on local or national issues?*

Q4. *List 3 local issues which you are interested in.*

Q5. *Is there any particular group of people who you are interested in working with (e.g., the elderly, the disabled, etc.)*

Q6. *What kind of skills do you have to offer? (Remember that even something like a driving licence can be important.)*

Q7. *What 3 national issues do you feel most strongly about? Do you already belong to, or have links with, groups which are taking up these issues?*

Q8. *Would you be prepared to put some money aside, either to help a cause or to provide you with information? If so how much?*

Q9. *What do other people think about your plans? How will they fit in with family life?*

Q10. *If you are a Christian, how do you think your choices should reflect your Christian faith?*

Q11. *To what extent are you prepared for your lifestyle to change if you are taking on an interest such as 'Green issues'?*

'i don't want to stand out from the crowd. If I do my friends will probably drop me because they think I'm weird or something.'

3

'I went out with a girl who called herself an "activist" once. If you didn't talk about "the cause" all the time she just wasn't interested.'

STANDING OUT IN THE CROWD

'As far as I can see there's no difference between a "Christian" view of housing and any other view. After all what does God know about living in rented accommodation?'

'I went on a march last week about increasing aid to the third world. Great fun. Only the guy walking alongside me was wearing a T-shirt with 'Trotsky Rules - O.K.' on it. I felt a bit uncomfortable. Was that wrong?'

going against the tide

It was a beautiful day in East Devon, England. The estuary was filled with people enjoying the sea. At this point of the coast the tide was strong but the water was shallow and reasonably safe. The favourite game was moving with the tide, floating on lilos and rubber tyres as the waves came higher and higher up the beach. From our vantage point on the top of the cliff, everybody was travelling with the tide in the same direction.

Except one. A lone swimmer was moving against the tide and was swimming strongly out to sea. Through the binoculars I could see the effort on the swimmer's face. I turned to Peter who lived in the village nearby. 'Who's the lone swimmer?' I asked. He looked through the binoculars. 'Her name is Christine Pascoe,' he said, 'she's a long distance swimmer who hopes to swim the channel in record time. This is how she trains. She builds up her strength by swimming against the tide.'

While Jesus calls Christian people to move against the tide, everybody prefers to take the line of least resistance: to do what comes easiest. But a part of counting the cost of discipleship is the struggle to go against the movement of the majority when they are endorsing wrong.

Christine Pascoe could only swim against the tide because she had determination and a goal. She didn't do it for fun. One of the big questions which faces us as Christians is 'How important is following Christ, to us?' Are we willing to lose a friend because we have views which are unfashionable? The Apostle Paul talks about 'pressing on towards the goal'. Some Christians are so easily distracted that they do not have a spiritual goal towards which they are aiming.

"...I felt a bit uncomfortable."

"Who's the lone swimmer?"

(Philippians 3:14)

We will need personal determination and spiritual power if we are to make headway against the spirit of the age.

It's not always going to be easy. Sometimes we feel like the man in the television advert who goes to a fancy dress party dressed as a chicken and flings open the door to find everybody in evening dress. Being a Christian can be costly.

But the cost is not always measured in persecution. In our image-conscious world being made to look foolish can be a sufficient deterrent to our standing up for the gospel.

God calls us to be Christlike. This does not mean that we have to adopt a certain hairstyle or one particular form of dress. What it does mean is that we reflect the mind and character of Christ and strive to become his physical presence in the world. He calls us to be integrated with the world but distinctive. And that can be hard.

"...and that can be hard."

$\mathcal{W}$ hat's the difference?

We know that Christian individuals are to be like Christ, but what about Christian policies? What is the difference between a housing policy drawn up by a Christian and one drawn up by anybody else? Surely when we get down to the policy level they're all much the same.

"What is the difference?"

There's some truth in this. Many of the policies which Christians arrive at by applying biblical principles to the situations we face, have been arrived at by other people by other means. But neglecting that stage of applying the relevant biblical principles would mean that Christians did not have any specific Christian basis for their actions. We'd simply be back following the crowd again.

Steps up the ladder. I like to think of the relationship of Christian ideals to policy as a ladder. At the top of the ladder there are specifically biblical ideals. As we come down the ladder there are perspectives derived from those ideals. At the bottom there are policies derived from those perspectives. Although the policies may not contain religious language it is still true that we have got there by 'thinking Christianly'. To miss out these steps would be disastrous and highly unchristian.

(Romans 12:1-2)

Of course there might be a number of policies which are compatible with those perspectives and we should expect that. We should also expect some healthy debate and disagreement between Christians on these things. After all, although the Bible is inspired, my interpretation of it isn't. It is very provisional. We must listen to, and learn from, each other.

So yes, Christian policies are distinctive, because they are derived from Christian thinking. But no, there is no one policy for every issue which is uniquely Christian. People who long for that are longing for the kingdom of God to come, and that will only happen when Jesus returns!

"...healthy debate..."

*b*eing taken over

Let's say that you have decided that you don't mind being known as a Christian and that a particular issue has grabbed your attention. There is one danger which it is important to note from the outset and that is being over-identified with the cause.

Some of the needs in our world have capacity to arouse our strongest emotions. The sight of people who are homeless or starving. The case of a child who has been abused by her parents. The injustice of racial discrimination. These are only some of the areas where we may feel justly angry.

Rightly so. But it is important to realize that the cause we serve is God's cause and that we believe that it is he who is in control and not us. If we lose sight of these two fundamental facts we might start to become obsessional about the cause.

From there it is a short step to becoming shortsighted and unfocused about other things. The more people are obsessed the more they lose their grip on a true perspective on life. Not only might you lose friends unnecessarily by becoming a bore but you might be a candidate for burnout and total exhaustion.

Other people can often judge better than you, whether the cause is dominating your life too much. The following things might happen:

- You dismiss the arguments of the opposition without giving them any consideration.
- You alienate other people by the intensity of your commitment.
- You want to talk about your pet subject all the time.
- You appear to judge others harshly if they are not interested in your cause.
- You are no longer interested in other people's interests.

*d*riven or called?

There is a considerable difference between being single-minded and being obsessional.

- Somebody who is single-minded knows their limitations. They have set certain goals which they can attain, but the obsessional person might set impossible goals. They then become driven by the unrealistic task they have set themselves.
- The single-minded person realizes that important as the cause is, life is also given by God to be enjoyed. They are liberated by God to

"...you might be a candidate for burnout..."

"...being single-minded and being obsessional..."

28

enjoy his world. He is in control not them. On the other hand the obsessional person might come to believe that if they don't do everything, it will not be done. They are driven by restlessness and possibly by guilt. In contrast, the single-minded person is not driven but feels the call of God on their life. They know that God will enable them to complete their task and derive great peace of mind from this.

(Philippians 1:6)

• The single-minded person brings the cause under the Lordship of Jesus Christ. However desperate the need, Christ comes first. They do not neglect their devotions nor meeting with other Christians for worship. The person who is obsessed may have first come to take action because of his faith but it was eclipsed long ago by the cause. Now it is the cause and not Christ which motivates him. His attitude to other Christians is one of anger and irritation that they do not share his passionate commitment and soon he stops attending church.

"...driven by restlessness..."

I have seen people become like this. Roger Burnett was somebody who became very committed to inner city mission. Others did not share his passion. He found himself more and more on the fringes of his church fellowship. They thought he wasn't 'sound'. Soon he found new friends in the local Labour Party who did share his convictions and he spent more time with them. The difference in this case was that he had too much self-respect to allow himself to get bitter. He simply drifted away.

When you are engaged in social action ask yourself frequently, *'Am I behaving as someone who is driven or called?'* If *you* don't know the answer your Christian friends will!

*M*arching with the Trots?

On some occasions we will find ourselves

"...fighting a common cause..."

agreeing with people over a specific issue, where normally, and more generally, we would disagree. Sometimes this might mean fighting in a common cause as allies. Christians have puzzled for years over the criteria for deciding when such *cobelligerence* (as it is called) is justified, and when it is not.

In one of the quotes at the top of this chapter the person who went on the march felt uncomfortable because she was side by side with a Trotskyite. It could equally have been somebody from the far right politically, or somebody who supports terrorist methods. But was this not a compromise of the gospel in some way?

This question is important and quite complicated. To start with let's distinguish between three scenarios where this problem might come up.
• Common concern
• Informal co-operation
• Formal coalitions

Common concern

All over the world people are concerned about human rights issues. Whether in the context of a right-wing dictatorship in Chile or the imprisonment of conscientious objectors in some Soviet bloc countries, many people in the free West feel that this infringement of civil liberties is an outrage.

"...human-rights issues."

Christians are to be clear about three things before they campaign.
• They must condemn all infringements of human rights whether they are carried out by left- or right-wing, friendly or unfriendly governments.
• They must be clear as to the biblical basis for human rights and the legitimate limitations of

human rights.

• They must be concerned that the methods they use in campaigning are as Christian as the ends they serve.

In such an issue the fact that Christians are concerned as well as all kinds of other groups is a matter of coincidence. There is a common concern. It may well be that many Christians will join an association like Amnesty International feeling that the cause is just and the methods used unproblematic.

Even at this broad level of nothing more than shared concern there may be problems. In recent years, to take another example, some Christians have felt so strongly about the siting of nuclear missiles at places like Greenham Common in Britain that they took part in direct action in order to try and remove the weapons. On occasion people climbed over or cut the fence surrounding the airbase in order to protest. Under the law they were at least committing trespass.

Law breaking. This raises an important question about the methods we can use as Christians. Is it permissible to break a perfectly reasonable law (the law of trespass), in order to draw attention to a policy with which you disagree? In other words, are Christians justified in taking the law into their own hands?

The answer must be no. In a democracy we agree that change comes *via* the ballot box. It may not happen to everybody's liking and some may believe the electoral system to be unfair, but if people took the law into their own hands anarchy would result.

You may feel strongly that the policy with which you disagree is morally wrong. Others feel the same way about legislation with which you can find no fault. If they have as much right

"...committing trespass."

(Romans 13:1)

as you to take the law into their own hands then civil society will break down. Our society depends on a commitment to the fact that the government has a right to govern us and to receive our taxes, *even if we disagree with its policies.*

Think about it. Presumably the leader of the opposition party pays his or her taxes like everyone else! A large proportion of those taxes go to pay for the very policies which he or she has opposed in Parliament.

"...Green issues..."

So even as we campaign for a just cause we must be careful that as we march alongside others who do not share our moral and spiritual world-view, we do not get drawn into using methods which are dishonouring to God.

*I*nformal co-operation

There are many issues on which Christians and other people are in substantial agreement. In many cases the thought and action of those who do not follow Christ is way ahead of that developed by Christians. Many of these concerns are expressed by Christians and others together without using any overtly religious language.

Such is the case with Green issues. If we put aside the methods used by Greenpeace activists which are sometimes controversial, many of the issues are naturally shared. We are concerned for the preservation of our world and repentant about our misuse of global resources.

(Genesis 2:15)

Of course when we are asked *Why?*, we will give different answers. Christians will look to God the Creator and to our responsibility as stewards for his world. Those of other faiths and none may be impressed by the empirical evidence and by the fact that we are borrowing resources that belong to our grandchildren.

We should not be surprised by such agreement. We are all made in God's image and that common image, though distorted, is still there. All human beings have some sense of justice and fairness, dignity and love. We might expect many Christians to be involved in the Green movement as a natural expression of their own concern for God's world.

Separate groups. This raises another question. Shouldn't Christians hive off and form their own Christian group? Not necessarily. It is, of course, important for there to be well-written Christian literature on a subject which draws out the Christian distinctives, but in the situation outlined above many Christians will choose to work within a broadly based open group.

There are situations where this is not easy in practice. Some groups working on the AIDS problem believe that active homosexual relationships are not only O.K. but should receive encouragement. On these kinds of issues it may be as well to demonstrate Christian caring for people living with AIDS, but to do so from within a specifically Christian network. This is not true of all AIDS groups, however, and some Christians are working successfully with hospices and networks to great effect, even though they have an ethos which is not Christian.

"...justice, fairness, dignity and love."

"...AIDS groups..."

It is important then to have a discerning eye for when the truth is being compromised. But there are many organizations doing a wonderful job which invite and deserve the support of everybody whatever their belief.

For this reason we have listed a whole range of such agencies in the user friendly guide at the back of this book. We leave the reader to decide how these principles are worked out within a particular group.

f ormal coalitions

In my dictionary, a coalition is defined as 'an alliance or union between groups, factions or parties, especially for some temporary or specific reason'.

Coalitions have a life and dynamic of their own as they are a form of public partnership. If the groups within them have different views of the world then the coalition may break down very quickly.

Coalitions are formed by negotiation. This can be a problem. If Christians form a coalition with groups who are unsympathetic to the gospel, who knows what might be demanded from them in negotiation? The rule is, therefore, only to form coalitions with those with whom one is in substantial agreement. If for some urgent reason or pressing cause, there is a need to spread the net more widely, then it must be only for that cause and no more. A church, for example, which becomes publicly or financially linked with an independent pressure group may find itself locked in to supporting practices with which it is unhappy.

"...be wary..."

This of course does not rule out *dialogue* with those with whom one disagrees. Such dialogue may open up the possibility of new areas of joint action. But Christians must be wary of giving 'any appearance of evil' or of compromising the gospel.

(1 Thessalonians 5:21-22)

Problems with other Christians. The label 'Christian' is applied to all kinds of groups and parties. Sadly the label is not enough to guarantee that people who carry it will agree or will find it possible to work together.

Throughout the world there are many 'Christian Democratic Parties' who have lost touch with their Christian roots. In documentary footage about the troubles in Beirut, reporters refer to 'Christian gunmen'. But even within the Christian church there is division on what being a Christian entails.

Perhaps it is helpful to ask the question, what is it that we are planning on doing together? If the joint activity is dependent on Christian belief and Christian doctrine then it may become an embarrassment to you and to others. There is little point in conducting evangelism with somebody who believes that 'everybody goes to heaven anyway'.

"...joint ventures..."

But if the joint venture is a practical act of service such as decorating the home of some disabled person or protesting about human rights then there may be every reason to suggest that it will go very well. Jesus told us to be 'as wise as serpents'. Let's remember that.

*d*oing good or serving God?

The 'throwing the baby out with the bathwater syndrome' is a very subtle problem even if it sounds a bit alarming. It happened to Guy Driscoll when he started to study law at university. Having been involved in his local community through a project in his school sixth form he came to university looking forward to getting stuck into social action with the Christian Union. Sadly he found that they were only into singing choruses and having the occasional speaker. They seemed to treat their time at university as a licence to ignore the community outside.

"It happened to Guy Driscoll..."

Guy was confused. He felt that social action was an important expression of the Christian gospel. He became aware that there was a Community Action group at the university which was very socially active and began to join in. Gradually his links with the Christian group lessened until he was only involved in community work. He ended up very confused and miserable feeling that he had done the wrong thing.

Guy had made the mistake of seeing social action as the most important aspect of Christian discipleship. I can understand his desire to do something. But our actions arise out of our convictions. We act like Christ because we imitate Christ and he is concerned for the whole person. Perhaps he would have been better off had he stayed in the Christian Union and tried to change it for the better.

Student Christian Unions are not primarily intended to organize social action. However, Guy's group should certainly have been more sympathetic and supportive of what Guy was burdened about even if it didn't actually set up the projects itself. He could have helped them to get out of their ghetto. However, despite the group's shortcomings, Christians like Guy must remember in every situation that *they do not serve good alone, but God alone*. This may sound like a cliché but it is an important truth.

"...real heartache..."

*g*o for what?

These problems of priorities can cause real heartache especially when Christians seem to be divided by them. We need to be so loving and open with those who differ from us.

One thing is sure. If you see your goal in purely human terms, it will begin to pall and weaken fairly soon. Whether we are visiting the elderly, campaigning for nursery provision, teaching English as a foreign language or doing debt counselling. It will all begin to get on top of us.

I have found it helpful at times like this to remember that what we are doing should be

"Would I still have treated her the same way?"

thought of in two ways.

• We are serving God. All we do is for him. I remind myself of what Jesus said. 'I tell you the truth, whatever you did for one of the least of these brothers of mine, you did for me.' What if that complaining old lady I visited had been Jesus? Would I still have treated her in the same way? Ask Jesus to fill you with a sense of his presence as you take action.

(Matthew 25:40)

• We are engaged in a spiritual struggle. We are working for the kingdom of God and will feel drained at times. Yet it is those who wait on the Lord who renew their strength. It is so vital not to neglect personal devotions or the fellowship of Christians. Action without prayer is unbelief.

(Isaiah 40:31)

God is at work with us in everything we do. Take courage from that to stand out in the crowd and so imitate Christ. This is the way our local, national and global life will be changed.

*'Work is
necessary for
man. Man in-
vented the
alarm clock.'*
Pablo Picasso
*'Work is the
expenditure of
energy (manual
or mental or
both) in the
service of
others, which
brings fulfil-
ment to the
worker,
benefit to the
community
and glory to
God.'*
John Stott

ACTION AT WORK

Many people are already doing those
things we are advocating as part of taking
action in the course of their paid employment. Health and Safety officials, environ-
mentalists, teachers, doctors, rubbish collectors
are all directly caring for the life and the shape
of the community we live in. It is important that
they see their job as Christian service because
if their standards are high then there will not
be as much need for others to patch up the
situations after them.

ACTION AT WORK

*W*hat are you doing?

In his book *Issues Facing Christians Today*, John Stott tells the following story: ... a man was taking a walk down a country lane when he came across a stone quarry in which a number of men were working. He questioned several of them about what they were doing. The first replied irritably, 'Can't you see? I'm hewing a stone.' The second answered without looking up, 'I'm earning £100 a week.' But when the same question was put to the third man, he stopped, put his pick down, stood up, stuck out his chest and said, 'If you want to know what I'm doing, I'm building a Cathedral.'

Even if the work we are doing is onerous, God is with us in it just as he has been with every slave who ever worked in chains. Our attitude can transform a difficult job into an act of worship.

Do you see what you are doing as a significant part of God's purposes? It may well be that in the most menial jobs where morale is low and resentment high, the Christian with this kind of attitude stands out from the crowd. Where the darkness is greatest the light is most visible.

"Can't you see? I'm hewing a stone."

(Ephesians 6:7)

*W*hat are you doing?

It is important then for people to study what they are doing. It may be that you are already involved in mission or service. I remember talking to one family doctor in Scotland who was too exhausted from all the pressure to be involved in Christian service in his church. his problem was that he saw his job as secular. He only started doing 'something for God' when he left his surgery. Yet the reason he was so tired was that he had spent all day caring for people.

Some people's problem is not that they are

"Where the darkness is greatest..."

so busy in their job that they have no time for spiritual things, *but that they have not begun to see their job as a spiritual thing.*

Others looking at their job will find it difficult to take this perspective. They only use a fraction of their potential in their work and are eager to get stuck in to additional responsibilities within the community. If they cannot share in a vision for their formal work they will work towards a vision for the community in another way.

So some need to wake up to the idea of their job as God's calling on their lives. Others need to discover a new contentment in a difficult situation through the grace of God. Yet many need to respond to the challenge of using the energy and potential which their job doesn't tap, in the service of the wider community.

"...it is possible to influence others..."

*P*ersonal influence

Whatever our work it is possible to influence others there. Where morale is low we can affirm and be positive. Where dishonesty is rife we can work with transparent integrity. Where there is resentment we can be gracious. Where standards are poor we can strive for excellence. There is no need to run with the crowd. Here is another situation where Christians are called to go against the tide.

It may be that the Christian entrepreneur can be extremely influential by sensitively using his or her wealth to create employment (and, indeed, a new sense of community self-respect) in an area which everyone else passes by. Where enterprise and entrepreneurship are placed at God's disposal in the service of his objectives, they can be powerful tools for good.

"...concerned about justice..."

But whatever our sphere of work it is important that we encourage and support those who work alongside us. The work situation can be a place where bored people gossip about others and where rumours spread like wildfire. These things are the refuge of the bored. Being salt and light in that situation means keeping confidences, and not passing on rumour.

Christians should also be concerned about justice issues at work. It is sometimes difficult to believe that the company which pays your wages is guilty of paying women half the man's pay for the same job, for instance. Others may find it difficult to pack cosmetics which have been devised in a process dependent on cruel, animal experimentation. We must not turn our backs on our responsibility to expose evil, even when the cost of doing so is high.

*P*eople and things

But for many workers, the issue is the physical quality of life at work rather than ethics. Our industrial society is geared to machines and computers much more than to people. But it is important to realize that an unhappy work-force is a product of poor management. And in purely money terms a resentful workforce will not be as productive as those included in on the decision making which affects them. Here is a basic lesson for managers and workers alike: *people matter more than things*. Any Christians wanting to be serious about their distinctive impact for Christ will build their management style on this principle of the workplace.

In the best-seller *In Search of Excellence* Thomas Peters and Robert Waterman looked at America's sixty-two most successful companies. They identified their success with the idea of 'shared values' which they found at the heart of such companies as *Coca-cola* and IBM. The goals, aspirations and methods of the company

"...America's sixty-two most successful companies."

were shared by everybody who worked for it.

Many people work in the opposite situation where facilities are poor and the management style is dictatorial. Christians should be in the vanguard of those seeking change. Taking action in this context might mean becoming an active trade-union official, or getting involved with health and safety issues at work. Here the Christian is seeking, not their own self-advancement, but justice and a better quality of life for others.

(Christian Impact has a lot of experience in helping people with professional problems as do ZADOK in Australia. Try also the UCCF in Leicester, UK.)

*r*esignation

The difficulties are not all on the side of the employee. Employers also wrestle with these problems. Some Christians go through torment when they have to make somebody redundant. They feel that there is little or no help for them in this difficult situation. Others find specific areas of corporate policy difficult to live with and struggle with the question: what is a resignation issue? People find that having a high regard for business morality is costly. You can only resign once. It is the ultimate weapon. When you have used it there is no guarantee that you will get another job.

So both Christian employers and employees are called to affirm 'good work' which incorporates teamwork in a culture of shared values. No Christian businessman should have a poor reputation. We must remember that in a fallen world profits are no guide to godly success. You can gain the whole world and still lose your own 'soul'. Our personal commitment is

"...the ultimate weapon."

to excellence because all we do we do for Christ. Our social commitment is justice for others.

So there are two distinct responses to an inadequate work situation. Firstly, Christians are called to inner contentment whatever state they find themselves in. We are not to be the one who pilfers, moans and backbites. But secondly, we are to work for change on behalf of others. Such change may be very costly.

Working in the home

Because status is distributed in our society *via* the pay-packet, those who work in the home often feel that they are neglected. They may work a lot harder than some highly paid professionals. Whether their task revolves around caring for elderly relatives or bringing up small children, or trying to manage a home full of adolescents with differing needs, they are always at their place of work.

Some people use their homes in very creative ways. Barbara is a childminder in our neighbourhood. Her home is a constant focus for young mums in the area. Not only does she free them to do other things and to get precious time for themselves, but they drop in for a cup of tea and a chat. The welcome is warm and the children cared for. This is taking action every bit as much as campaigning for an improved home for the elderly.

Others offer hospitality to the lonely by inviting people for meals or to go on walks. Still others go further and put their spare room to good use by inviting people to stay when they are going through difficulties.

the family

Others become foster parents, looking after

(Matthew 16:26)

"...justice for others."

"...abolished childhood..."

children who are suffering from rejection and abuse. Some willingly accept the pain of fostering a baby who is HIV positive. Still others adopt a child when they could have one more of their own, because they want to do something for those who feel unwanted.

The key to the use of the home is that it is a resource which can be used for more people than the immediate family. But if it is to be used in this way the whole family must be involved. If the homeworker gets lumbered with it all, it just adds another problem.

Perhaps your home might be a little more open? It could be used for coffee mornings, schools association meetings, prayer groups, evangelistic suppers, fellowship groups, meetings of the local disability group or political party, or...

Make your home a home for anyone who needs it.

*C*ommon concern

A voluntary agency is a self-governing group of people who have joined together to take action for the improvement of the community and not for financial reward. There are over 550,000 such groups in the UK.

The National Council for Voluntary Organizations represents such agencies and if you want to find out what the possibilities are in your locality then going to the NCVO is a good place to start. They will give you an interview and discuss the kinds of areas in which you are interested. Information and many publications about their nationwide work can be obtained from their national address. (See 'The user-friendly guide'.)

Several of the groups that have emerged from this voluntary network are very large and

"...fostering a baby who is HIV positive."

(Acts 2:42-47)

"...a good place to start."

include Charities Aid Foundation, National Association of Citizens Advice Bureaux and Age Concern.

If you wish to work for a specifically Christian organization then there are many to choose from. *The UK Christian Handbook* contains thousands of addresses and descriptions of such organizations. The Evangelical Alliance will be able to help you with the activities of its member groups. It exists to link Christians together and represent them to the wider world. Your local church leader might also know of local groups.

Whether you are interested in politics, industrial relations, prison visiting, disability or campaigning, there is probably a Christian group geared up to help you.

One last point which follows on from what we said at the opening of this chapter: work is not the same as employment. If you are unemployed that does not mean you cannot still derive dignity and self-worth from working for the community. Voluntary work is a very good way of doing that. Of course there are problems when you are also trying to find a new job but many people are in need of the skills that you represent and even if you can only help them for a week you will have made a difference to somebody else's life.

"...there are many to choose from."

"...you will have made a difference..."

'i don't understand politics. I've never been outside my country, even for a holiday.'

'I go into my school regularly and

CHAPTER

help out, I visit the elderly and am involved in an attempt to get nursery provision in our area. You asked me if I was involved in mission. Isn't that mission?'

5

COMMUNITY ACTION

'Our area doesn't feel like a community. Everybody keeps themselves to themselves. They all pretend to be happy. But the divorce rate is high and a lot of people seem to be on an awful lot of pills. Surely we could do something to break down the barriers between people?'

What kind of community?

Where I come from the word 'community' is a 1980s over-used word. That is to say that people throw it around without much thought to what it means. In this chapter it simply means the locality in which you and I live. The problem many of us have is that our lives are spinning so fast that we don't know very much about our local area. Others, like the old lady who used to live down the road from me until she died last year, know everything there is to know about the locality, but have no-one to whom they can pass on their wisdom and no real sense of being able to bring about change.

"..do you actually know what goes on around you?"

Before taking any kind of action in the community it is important to survey the area. It may sound ridiculous but do you actually *know* what goes on around you? Walk the streets and talk to people. Ask questions (such as those listed in the 'Workbench' section at the end of this chapter).

Ask yourself what facilities the community lacks. Listen to the moans of local people. Are there a lot of mums with young children but no nursery facilities? Why not? There must be a story there somewhere? Your local councillor might be able to help.

When churches do these kind of surveys to find out about their area, they are called church audits and most denominations have people who can come alongside a church to do one. The reason you are asking these questions is that you are not assuming you know the needs or the profile of your community. The rule is *listen*, don't impose. (See Fran Beckett's book *Called to Action*.)

"...church audits..."

$\mathcal{W}$ hat kind of opportunities?

Your survey might throw up all kinds of possibilities. There might be one obvious need which stands head and shoulders above all the rest. Mary Hill surveyed her area and found that it had a very high unemployment rate. She

"...a real headache..."

also found that there were no facilities for the use of unemployed people during the day. She took up their cause and, as a result of lobbying by unemployed people with her help, sports facilities and an unemployment 'drop in' club were provided.

Locally speaking

Local libraries are very good sources of information. They will have a section devoted to the local area and statistics compiled by the local council which will help you to get a feel for the area.

Perhaps you have one institution which dominates the area. Phil and Janet Higginson live just by the local prison. They regarded this as a real headache until they saw the possibilities of getting involved in visiting. They contacted the Prison Christian Fellowship and were soon visiting and helping those living in the prison community. For them their local area provided the clue as to what they should do to take action.

"...the faces are always changing."

It's not only important to ask questions about the community. Another important question is: are you a person whose life is focused on the local community? Many people who feel at sea when 'national' issues are raised, feel quite at home chatting about what's going on around them. They live and work in the community. This is especially true of women who work in the home.

Others commute to work outside their local community. They may even use their own homes as 'bed and breakfast' stop-overs between work sessions. Their focus is found wherever their work takes them. They may make occasional use of their community but they will probably not get involved in the detail of what makes it tick.

Others are in transition. They may be seasonal workers in rented accommodation or students who are only present for part of the year. Tourists also swell the local population at certain periods. Such people have needs and yet they may turn over very fast. The community has the same type of people in it but the faces are always changing.

So a survey, either of the informal personal variety or of the more formal church 'audit', will pinpoint strategic possibilities. The right people to respond to these opportunities are those who know the community best and they may be just the people who feel most powerless when it comes to taking action.

"...as parents we have rights..."

*L*ocal schools

Those people who send their children to local schools will be presented with several opportunities to take part in community affairs.

It is, of course, as parents that we have rights in the school context. Our influence for good can be considerable especially at the primary level. Parents who are positive and have ideas are nearly always welcomed by schools which are under-resourced. Teachers often welcome parents who will come into school to help out. This might mean working in the classroom listening to children reading, helping with displays, or with some aspect in which the parent has expertise (*e.g.* music, art or sport).

Gifts of books or apparatus may also be welcomed. Take advice before you do anything. If a Parent Teachers Association or Parents Club is meeting, get involved. But do not get involved in the life of a school unless you have the best interests of the children at heart.

Involvement may lead to becoming a school governor in the UK or a school council member

"...become a parent governor..."

in some parts of Australia. In the UK since the 1988 Education Reform Act, this is an important and powerful responsibility. It will involve quite a time commitment including training sessions for governors and may involve taking time off work. It may be that you should see this as your main area of Christian service. All parents are eligible to become a parent governor of a school where their child is a pupil.

To be elected you will need to be proposed and seconded by other parents and then will need to do some public relations in your area. In Britain you can also be elected a school governor by the Local Education Authority or by being co-opted by the other governors. You would serve for a period of four years.

"...recent changes in education."

Information about becoming a governor can be obtained from your local education authority. (See also the section on education in 'The user-friendly guide'.)

If you want one book to read on the current educational situation from a Christian perspective, then it would be difficult to better *Schools Now: A Parent's Guide* by Charles Martin. He has had thirty years of experience in teaching and was principal of Bilborough College in the UK for twelve years. His wisdom is profound and the book reflects helpfully on recent changes in education. In Australia a useful resource is the *Journal of Christian Education* available from AFES (see 'The user-friendly guide').

Lastly, it is important to remember that a school is itself a community and for those who attend it provides one of the most important formative influences in their whole life. Becoming involved in the process of guiding and forming the next generation is an important calling whether it be as teacher, governor or informal helper.

*g*etting into housing

Unemployment is often cited as the statistic which provides a barometer of the social misery in our country, but housing also is in a mess. In the UK the housing market is inefficient due to the operation of the rent acts, subsidies to council house rents, tax relief on mortgages and planning regulation.

Arthur Jesmond got involved in a Christian housing association when he found himself looking for housing between jobs. He found a split between housing which was far too expensive and housing which was not fit to live in. There was little or no housing to rent. Eventually after a period of some desperation he found a home through a housing association. As someone with management experience he became interested in the way they operated and found himself involved in housing provision and, in his case, counselling those with housing needs

Information about housing associations can be obtained from the National Federation of Housing Associations, and other relevant literature can be obtained from The National Federation of Housing Co-operatives.

Those interested in sheltered housing for those with handicaps of any sort or in housing for the elderly should contact the Shaftesbury Society.

Those interested in housing as an educational issue should contact Shelter who have audio-visual resources and simulation games. The Evangelical Urban Training Project (EUTP) also has a walkabout exercise to help you understand the meaning of the housing situation in your neighbourhood.

*h*omeless

Any interest in housing *should* also lead to an

"Arthur Jesmond got involved..."

"...simulation games..."

*"He always
used to feel
guilty about
homeless
people..."*

interest in homelessness. All too often this is not the case. Homeless people suffer from more stereotyping than almost any other single group. Anything I say will be inadequate. What I can say is that Patrick Logan's book *A life to be lived: homelessness and pastoral care* is an excellent practical handbook for those who wish to take action in this area.

Nicholas Piper works as a volunteer in the local night shelter for homeless people. He always used to feel guilty about homeless people especially those he saw as 'tramps'. One day he saw the church administrator writing out a small yellow ticket and giving it to somebody who looked in need of a good meal. The administrator explained that it was a voucher for the local cafe at the shelter for homeless people. From that time Nick carried a supply of the vouchers and when approached was able to give one away. This solved his problem of giving money which could have been spent on drink.

When he went to the shelter to get the tickets he met people who seemed ordinary enough. When a chance to give a few hours of his time came up he offered his services and has now been working there for a few months. He really seems to have found a ministry.

Help on housing can be got from Shelter, CHAR (Campaign for the Rootless and Homeless), National Youth Bureau, Leaving Home Project, HASSLL (Homeless against Social Security Lodging Laws). Telephone advice in the London Area can be had from the Housing Advice Switchboard, 01 434 2522.

*W*elfare and need

It has often been said that we have a welfare state because we have failed as a welfare society. Christians have also been accused of only being concerned for the 'spiritual' side of life rather than being concerned about the quality of people's lives while they are alive.

Most modern societies such as France, Australia and Britain have highly developed welfare systems. Our problem is that no system can deliver love. If there are resources available the system can attend to the survival needs of people, though there are still major injustices as in the case of homeless people.

But people want to be drawn into *relationships*. We are all as sensitive to the attitude of the person who hands over our benefit as we are to the amount of the benefit itself.

Taking action in the area of welfare opens up a vast sphere of human need. Firstly, which group? The person in debt? The old lady being threatened by her landlord? The unmarried mum who can't cope? Colin, the depressed young man in his twenties who has not been in work for a year? Or Phil, who has just been released into the community by the local psychiatric hospital and spends his time walking the streets bewildered, because he is turned out of his B&B accommodation all day?

All these people need more than the system can offer them. The problem is that there are two forms of help which can be offered. The first treats everybody's needs as identical. Food, clothing, shelter, etc. This kind of help can be delivered by a system. But there is another kind of help. Each person can be treated as an individual with their own personal needs and a story which must be listened to with sympathy and care. Such help can be found only within human relationships.

*i*n need of love

Where are those in need to turn to for such love, given the demands on every part of the welfare

"...no system can deliver love."

"...more than the system can offer..."

"...welfare-rights advice..."

system? We are told that our communities are fragmenting and that we are not as friendly as we used to be. Surely this should be the focus of the church's mission in the world – to show people the love of Christ in practical ways which make a difference to the quality of their lives.

Again there is great scope for individuals offering their service through the National Council for Voluntary Organisations, but there is also a role for the church. Many churches are now setting up welfare-rights advice work because of the real need in their area.

Credit

In some churches this is associated with debt counselling for those who are in debt difficulties. Other churches are forming credit unions. These are groups which run like a co-operative bank. Some put money in, others take it out. They make the decisions about where the money goes. They run it. Sometimes it can bring new hope to a housing estate. Often they are focused on a church and are run from the church hall. Through them people can borrow money at low interest rates because their overheads are low.

"...credit unions..."

Still others are forming housing associations or using government grants to set up employment schemes or build small workshops. In some urban areas the church is now acknowledged as one of the prime movers for change in the community.

When people and communities have been destroyed by social blight, they are not healed by money being thrown around. It is by listening to their needs and acting appropriately in the light of what they say that change can come about gradually. Then money can be used wisely to serve people at the point of need.

*Y*our local Member of Parliament

There are many reasons for wanting to see your local MP, including getting him or her on your side in a local dispute, complaining about government policy or even to offer a compliment on his or her latest speech!

But you may also wish to see your MP because you would like to see a change in the law. If you want to do this you will probably need the support of your local MP.

MPs promise to serve the entire constituency (the area which elects them) and not just those who voted for them. It doesn't matter then whether you are a member of their party or not. They are still there to serve your interests, not their own. They are our representatives. MPs are only as good as their information. In the case of their constituency they are only as good as their local information. *They need you.*

They also cannot sort out problems which they don't know exist. So go and see them.

You can write to them at the House of Commons, asking for an appointment to see them there. Alternatively you can meet at the local constituency office. All MPs have 'surgeries' where they meet constituents to discuss problems.

Precise questions. It helps if you have prepared a 'brief' beforehand. Even better if you have sent it on to your MP in advance of the meeting. To tell an MP that 'something is wrong' or 'something should be done about X' is to waste their time. They will want to act, but to enable them to do this they will need a clear brief. Prepare some questions and answers on no more than one piece of A4 paper. Ask yourself

"They are still there to serve your interests..."

"What would it cost?"

the following questions:
- What is the present situation?
- Why should it be changed?
- Who is suffering damage or loss?
- Are you alone in this view – if not who are your supporters?
- What do you recommend should be done?
- What would be the result of your proposed action?
- Who would benefit and who would lose?
- What would it cost?

One good concise piece of supporting documentation will help. But keep it brief.

Your MP will take your case seriously if you approach him or her properly. If it concerns welfare – housing, health or money – he or she will probably act quickly. If it is a political issue he or she may well take that up on your behalf. Remember that an MP will not act against his or her own declared beliefs. If you go to a Tory MP with a brilliant plan to renationalize an industry which has just been privatized I suggest you might just be wasting your time.

"...time to think..."

Don't expect too much from a first meeting, especially if it is at a busy 'surgery'. Leave your brief, having made your case, and make another appointment. Your MP will need time to think the matter through and perhaps consult with others.

*f*urther action

Assuming your MP takes your case or problem or proposal on board, what can he or she do next?
- Write to or see the Minister concerned or table a parliamentary question to the responsible minister.
- Raise the matter in a debate or an adjournment debate.
- Table amendments to a proposed bill or

introduce a private member's bill.

Of course some of these things are highly unlikely. It is also true that it helps if your MP is a member of the government. So there are limits to what he or she can do or is willing to do. Nevertheless, MPs are our representatives and do wield power in our democracy.

More information on all aspects of lobbying and parliamentary procedure are contained in Ian Greer's book *Right to be Heard*. Care Campaigns also publish a useful manual on campaigning in the UK which includes a lot of information about approaching one's MP.

*d*oing good or serving God?

Councillors have the interest of the locality at heart. In the UK there are several different kinds of councillor. They have different kinds of responsibility. The first tier is the parish councillor with responsibility for things such as footpaths running through the locality.

The next tier is the district councillor who has responsibility for setting the community charge (poll tax). Housing is one of the most important areas here. A district council holds its own housing stock and acts as landlord. It has obligations under the law and must also provide for the homeless.

Planning is another area. It is under this heading that councillors meet subjects such as Sunday Trading. If a hypermarket asks for planning permission for an out of town site then the planning permission has to go through the district council. Enforcement of Sunday Trading laws is also in the hands of the council.

Environmental concerns such as the emptying of rubbish bins, dog dirt, salmonella in milk and eggs and the monitoring of public health are also important. One local council recently

"...a steel bolt was found in a loaf of bread!"

prosecuted a well known supermarket chain when a steel bolt was found in a loaf of bread! One Christian district councillor said that he saw his job as concerned with the immediate quality of day to day life of people in the district.

The county council is responsible for large scale spending on services organized on a county-wide basis. Social services, education, emergency services, environmental issues and libraries are among these. The County Council also sets a local charge which is collected through the district councils. All councillors are on a committee. It is left to the political parties to allocate the places on the committee to members. Places are determined by the size of party.

It is in the committee that the individual councillor can be at his or her most effective. In the chamber they may be a back-bencher with little power but in the committee they will often be able to exert more influence. The most important person on any committee is the chairperson who controls the agenda. If you have an issue you wish to be discussed then it first has to get onto the agenda and that may not be easy!

"Doris had a major problem with her house..."

*t*he story of Doris

Doris had a major problem with her house which was part of the council housing stock. She was seventy-three and couldn't do very much for herself. Her house was in an appalling state. When the man from the council came round to see the problems he told her she should be in a home, which upset her. Her neighbour saw her local councillor who decided to take up her case. He got no help from the officials concerned and tried to get it onto the agenda of the committee responsible for housing repairs. The chairperson would not allow it onto the agenda.

The councillor went round his colleagues but they had enough trouble without this hot potato. In the end the councillor had to argue the case in the full council and propose a motion which was passed by the whole council which said that it must be placed on the agenda of the relevant committee. By the time all this had happened and before the repairs could be carried out the old lady died.

*L*ocal lobbying

In many cases local politics is about knowing who has the power and developing access to them. Effectiveness in lobbying is always about being able to reach the person who matters, and who can make the necessary changes. Even councillors (especially if they are in opposition) may find it difficult to make headway. It is important to say that just because your councillor is a Christian doesn't mean that he or she is more skilled in this respect.

Those who see the local area as the area for action will sooner or later wish to lobby the council. I asked a well known local councillor where Christians could make a difference. He thought that in the area of planning applications and in housing there was a lot of room for well-informed lobbying. With recent legislation in the UK and the possible sale of housing estates to private landlords it is important for housing action groups to be vigilant.

Local action achieves more for the amount of pressure exerted than national action. Local churches know their area well and have a network of local contacts. Indeed the church might have a better network than anyone else. Many

"...well-informed lobbying."

"...mission must be expressed politically."

political parties will only have a few people.

Some churches ought to seriously consider whether Christians in the congregation have a calling to stand as councillors. This would not be to represent the church but to do a good job as a councillor. After all, mission must be expressed politically. All churches ought to develop links and support the work of their local councillor.

*t*aking local action

So you thought you were of no use because you were a small-minded person. You thought that just because you didn't understand the big political debates you couldn't exert influence. But if you care about your local community then you can make a tremendous difference to the quality of life of the people who live there. That is Christian service.

"Listen to the pulse-beat of the community."

So get involved. Take a trip to your local library. Begin to talk to local church leaders, pay a visit tot he offices of your local newspaper, go to the surgery of your local MP or councillor. But go listening. Don't go with a ready-mixed agenda. Listen to the pulse beat of the community. Build up a picture of the needs. Ask yourself how you with others can meet that need. Imagine the excitement when you get your first victory. I suspect that not only will you change the life of your community, but your life will be changed as well.

WORKBENCH

Asking the right questions

These questions are for a home group to work through in your locality. They are drawn from material used in conducting church audits. Spend several weeks gathering the material, giving people different sections to concentrate on. Then spend an evening or, even better, a day away together looking at the profile of your area which you have put together.

This should be something that you enjoy doing!

This approach does not ask questions of individuals in the street. If you want to conduct a more in-depth survey of people's views then you can use a community survey such as the one in Fran Beckett's book, Called to Action *(pp. 212-214).*

Questions

Q1. *What are the natural boundaries in your area (e.g. rivers, canals, busy main roads, railways, etc.)?*

Q2. *What are the political boundaries (e.g. ward, district, etc.)?*

Q3. *How many churches operate in your area? What are they? How many people attend? What community facilities do they offer?*

Q4. *What kind of housing is in your area (you will need to go into detail in this section): council or private; rented or owner occupied; good condition or poor condition; old or new? Use somebody with photographic skills to provide a record.*

Q5. *How is the trend changing with respect to housing? (For instance, are young families moving in and 'doing up houses' or are slums being cleared or office space replacing living accommodation?)*

Q6. *What is the area like with respect to policing and crime? (Talk to the local community police.) Are there Neighbourhood Watch schemes in operation? Who runs them?*

Q7. *What kind of schools does the area have? How*

"What are the moans?"

resourced? What are their needs. (Talk to teachers and to the head as well as school governors.)

Q8. What kind of welfare provision is there? Talk to the local Citizens Advice Bureau, the local Councillors and your local MP. Where are people falling through the systems and not being cared for?

Q9. Where do people meet? (Pubs, clubs, community centre, bingo, etc.) Who uses them? Is there a tradition of 'helping one another'? Does a 'Good Neighbour' scheme operate?

Q10. What kind of people live in the community? (Age groups, ethnic backgrounds, class and social groupings.) What kind of turnover is there in the area?

Q11. What facilities exist for people? (Parks, gyms, luncheon clubs, cinema, theatre, music, evening classes, libraries, swimming pools, dancing/discos, nightclubs, restaurants.)

Q12. Do you have large institutions in your area which dominate local life? (Hospitals, prisons, factories, etc.) How do people relate to them?

Q13. What are the moans and the comments of small businesses/shops in your area?

Q14. What kind of medical provision do you have in your area? (Family doctor, chemist, community psychiatrist, community midwife, etc.) Are these services adequate?

Q15. Do people regard the churches in the area positively? How do they view them?

Q16. How can you match the needs arising from your survey with the gifts and abilities of those in your home group or church?

This should provide you with a lot of material which should be very interesting. Combine it with photographs, graphs, reports from local newspapers (don't forget to talk to them!), to provide you with an entertaining presentation. The aim is to make you more aware of what is going on around you so that your prayer, mission and Christian service actually meet the needs of people around you.

If you want to do more than this you will need help.

You will always need help if you are going to conduct a full scale church audit of your area. If you are an Anglican write to your local Diocesan office which will have information if not audit packs. Otherwise write to denominational headquarters. Baptists, United Reformed and Methodists have all produced packs and have people to help. Have a good time!

'the most success-ful politician is he who says what every-body is think-ing most often and in the loudest voice.'
Theodore Roosevelt

'I could not be leading a

CHAPTER

6

religious life unless I ident-ified myself with the whole of mankind, and that I could not do unless I took part in poli-tics.'
M. K. Gandhi

THE NATIONAL SCENE

'Television is an invention that permits you to be entertained in your living room by people you wouldn't have in your home.' **David Frost**

*N*ational politics – the big time

David and Tricia Graham were known for their lively supper parties. At one of these, which was made up of some of their Christian friends, the conversation got round to politics. Soon the fur was flying. People were calling politicians all kinds of names, making hasty judgments on very little information and stereotyping anybody who looked as if they might disagree with them.

'I suddenly got very fed up,' Dave told me later. 'Here we were behaving like a bunch of seven-year-olds. The heated conversation seemed to say that this was something that people cared about, yet none of us had ever done anything about our convictions.'

The conversation changed to a more constructive discussion about why people were not interested in getting involved in politics. Tricia said, 'Shouldn't we *do* something, rather than having silly arguments?' Everyone agreed.

*The continuing story...*They decided to meet the next Saturday. When they got together Dave had prepared some questions for them to ask themselves.

From discussing those questions they concluded that those of them who were bored didn't really understand what was going on in the country. They didn't understand how Parliament operated or any of the major problems facing MPs. So they decided to meet again and to get some information.

They also decided that being Christians meant that they should rethink their politics from first principles.

This debate was quite heated. One of them, Tony Drew, saw Christianity as having nothing to do with politics. He withdrew from the group when he saw the direction it was taking for the very positive reason that he valued their friendship and wanted to retain it. He wished them well in their new pilgrimage and left.

The first thing that some of the group did was to change their newspaper so that they

"calling politicians all kinds of names..."

"...some of the group changed their newspaper..."

"...anybody with a bit of sense could get involved..."

could read more seriously about what was going on. Others began to read a news weekly. Others found out about how Parliament operates. One or two of them found out a little information about how to lobby an MP or write to a government Minister.

They began to meet every fortnight, have something to eat and then share what they had found out since they last met. One or two dropped out but the majority began to be fascinated by what they were learning.

Several things happened.

1. They stopped putting people with whom they disagreed in boxes. They began to respect the views of the opposition. They learned about the history of the position which Tony Drew had taken and learned to respect that option as well.

2. They began to want to pray for those with responsibility who had tough decisions to make.

3. They began to want to *do* something because they saw that *anybody* with a bit of sense could get involved and make a difference.

4. They decided to go and meet their MP as soon as they could, at the House of Commons.

*t*ea at the Commons

So they wrote to their MP and asked her if she could get them tickets for the 'Strangers Gallery' at the House of Commons and would she be willing to meet with them for half an hour?

They were delighted to get tickets and to be given an appointment for tea with their MP!

Her advice was something like this.

1. They could each join their local party. These were often desperate for help.

2. They could find an issue which interested them and work for change through an organiz-

"They could find an issue which interested them..."

ation which worked in that area. This would inevitably have a political element.

3. They could offer to share their new-found knowledge in the local secondary school or sixth form college.

4. They could write letters on related issues to the press or to MPs or to Ministers, including the Prime Minister.

5. They might even wish to consider standing for Parliament themselves or becoming a local councillor.

6. They could use their vote wisely (and vote for her at the next election!).

She was also honest enough to say that politicians didn't always know what to do in tough situations. She quoted Sir Paul Chambers, a famous industrialist, who had said that 'exhortation to other people to *do something* is the last resort of politicians who are at a loss to know what to do themselves'! Sometimes this leads to 'a lot of hot air'.

"I asked Dave what happened to the group."

ƒ our golden rules

After the meeting they reviewed what they had learned. Four golden rules seemed to stand out clearly.

1. Don't be ignorant or prejudiced – be well informed.

2. Learn about how politics ticks.

3. Develop a relationship, either by letter or a visit, with your MP.

4. When you see a problem in society don't just treat the symptoms. Ask how the cause of the problem can be dealt with.

I asked Dave what had happened to the group. He said that one person was now deeply involved with Friends of the Earth, another had changed jobs and was working as a race relations officer for an Anglican Diocese; one of the teachers was now taking current affairs in her sixth form and was doing very well and they were all quite involved in their local parties although some of them found the low attendance and the poor quality of debate quite depressing.

'What is the main thing you've learned?' I asked him. 'Cynicism is a luxury for those who aren't involved', he replied, after some thought.

He admitted that politics was sometimes difficult to understand, but Christians are committed to truth rather than short-cuts.

He also let me have one or two of the letters he had written to 'bigwigs' which I found interesting because they showed me how to approach writing such a letter myself. I noticed that they were typed and on headed notepaper. Both of which add a bit of authority.

Here's one which was addressed to the Prime Minister, so the envelope was addressed to Rt Hon Mrs M. Thatcher MP. (If it had been to an MP it would have started 'Dear Mr ...')

"...committed to truth rather than short-cuts."

Rt Hon Mrs M. Thatcher MP
10 Downing St,
London SW1

Dear Prime Minister,

As a group of concerned Christians from all parties we are writing to you about the escalation of the personal debt crisis which is sweeping our country.

In particular, we are concerned about the practice of 'redlining' postal districts so that people in poor areas cannot get loans in the formal financial sector. This means that people resort to moneylenders who are charging rates which are extortionate. This is sometimes accompanied by coercion of the borrower.

We ask that the government pass legislation which places ceilings on interest so that interest *rates of 80% cannot be charged. Secondly, we ask that all companies which advertise loans are statutorily obliged to describe* in plain language which is easily readable *the conditions for the loan and the Annual Percentage Rate which applies.*

We would draw your attention to the points made by the Familybase *movement in their literature. We enclose a copy of their 'CRASH' programme with which we are fully in agreement.*

We are sending copies of this letter to the Chancellor of the Exchequer, the Minister for Consumer Affairs and our local MP.

Thank you for taking the time to deal with this request.

Yours sincerely...

This may not be a perfect letter but it did produce a response from the Prime Minister's Office and later in the year, partly as a result of people like them writing to Ministers, and also as a result of others highlighting the debt problem, the Minister for Consumer Affairs did introduce new legislation about the advertising of loans.

Now *that's* taking action.

g oing further

Some people reading this will find such advice simplistic in the extreme. Fair enough. You will need a more comprehensive guide to what goes on in Parliament. You will want to know how to find out about MPs' interests (including religious affiliations), who sits on what committees, news about prospective legislation and how to apply pressure on the parliamentary process. So if you are already quite sophisticated in your approach – good news! – a book exists which may meet all your needs. It's called *Lobbying: An Insider's Guide to the Parliamentary Process* and it's written by former

"...how to apply pressure on the parliamentary process."

MP, Alf Dubs. MP Joan Ruddock says of it on the back cover, 'Some MPs will hate this book. It is more revealing about Parliament than television will ever be.' Its strength is in showing you where and how to exert pressure. (Sell your shirt to buy it!)

W riting to the media

How do you respond to what you watch on your television? Perhaps you don't respond at all.

The one relevant fact that should get us actively responding to television is the statistic that one letter written to the television networks to complain or praise is counted as 1,000 viewers. Now imagine what would happen if your whole church could be persuaded to write to the BBC, IBA or Australia's ABC about something. It might actually cause quite a stir!

Next time you see something on television that you wish to respond to, write there and then to the producer of the programme concerned. If you want to be sure about the address then you could telephone to find out the exact location of the office concerned. Remember that local stations in Britain (such as Central or Yorkshire) are especially interested in feedback from those areas.

There are also several programmes devoted to feedback. Most channels on radio and TV have some kind of programme where people can telephone or write in and make their point.

"...write to the BBC, IBA or Australian ABC."

Write to be heard. Here are some pointers about what to say.

1. Always write a short letter. Make your point succinctly.

2. Don't quote obscure Bible texts at people. Your letter might be filed in the waste paper bin! Identifying yourself as a Christian is OK

(although not always necessary) but have you made your point in such a way that a person who is not a Christian can understand and even sympathize with it?

3. It would be good if Christians wrote in to praise as well as complain sometimes. After all what do we stand for? (They know what we're against.)

4. If possible try to write on subjects other than those which Christians are generally known to be concerned about (sex, obscenity, violence). These are of course of vital importance, but we do need to demonstrate our concern for other kinds of issues as well.

"Make your point succinctly."

Here are some issues which should concern us.

• *Just reporting.* Are racial minorities correctly represented in the media? Are inflammatory situations (Beirut, Northern Ireland, etc.) fairly reported?

• *Insensitive intrusion.* Television can sometimes be overly intrusive in times of catastrophe or grief. Privacy needs to be respected.

• *Political bias.* Are all sides of an important argument being represented?

• *Advertising.* Surely as Christians we should be protesting very loudly at some of the advertising which pours into our homes. The images portrayed can be especially powerful.

If you have a home group it makes a good exercise to draw up a list of those things which you feel should be monitored in the media.

Of course the media are not only there for us to monitor but also for us to use as a means of taking action. You may wish to use them to get your message across.

"...the media are ... a means of taking action."

*h*ow to watch television

If you do form a group, for instance, whether it is an independent group for your own interest or whether it is attached to one of the national agencies, you may be more effective in your dealings with the media than if you only have your own personal resources to draw on.

• You can appoint somebody to monitor television, radio and newspapers on a rota basis.

• You can organize a letter-writing campaign where many people write in about the same issue. (They should always use their own words.)

• You can organize articles for your local press on specific issues.

• You can attend 'Question Time' programmes and request tickets for the group. You may be asked for a question or comment.

• You can issue press releases on behalf of the group. To do this make sure you know the deadlines for the papers or programmes you are interested in catching. (It helps if you have a Press Officer, headed paper and a contact telephone number. It also helps if the group has a name!)

In this instance it is important that you stand for something positive as a group. It is also important that those who don't understand religious language can understand and sympathize. If you are a group of inarticulate moaners you will get nowhere (and quite rightly so!).

In any debate think through the one point which you wish to make. Illustrate it with anecdotes or statistics and make it. Do not waffle on.

Some agencies exist just to monitor the press and the media in general. I rang David Houghton, Deputy Director of the Broadcasting Standards Council and asked him to explain what they did and how concerned Christians could link in with their work. Its brief is to consider violence, sex, taste and decency. It also covers satellite transmissions. There are eight members of the council and their first job has been to draw up a code of practice for the broadcasting industry as a whole.

"Do not waffle on."

They consider complaints about programmes from the general public, undertake research, produce an annual report and report regularly to the Home Secretary.

They are obviously a key target for Christian comment and opinion. Their address is in 'The user-friendly guide'.

A leaflet can be obtained from them which explains what they do more fully and gives guidelines about making complaints.

It is as well to say that, at the time of writing, they have very few teeth. They can advise but little else. If public opinion does not get behind them then they will become yet another agency that nobody listens to. That would be a missed opportunity.

Other bodies exist such as The Press Council and The Advertising Standards Authority in the UK and Justice in Broadcasting and The Children's TV Foundation in Australia to whom individuals can write with complaints and comments. Details can be found in 'The user-friendly guide'.

"But the media can act as our champion."

*i*nvestigative journalism

Until now we have looked at monitoring the media itself or using the media to represent our message. But the media can act as our champion. The tradition of investigative journalism can, at its very best, be a crucial guardian of individual freedom and dignity. There are any number of programmes which will take up the cause of people who have been wronged. Of course, the seamy side of investigative journalism as represented by many of the tabloid newspapers is something which we need to resist and condemn.

It's important that we expose injustice wherever we find it. In our society there is no better way of bringing things to light than exposing them on national television. Such programmes frequently invite people to write to them with their stories and if you know of somebody who is suffering an injustice and cannot get redress through other channels it may well be effective for the media to take up the issue.

In this chapter we have deliberately set involvement in formal politics and involvement in the media side by side. There are some people who would say that the latter is more effective in a world where people are cynical about politics. I disagree. Both have a vital place. They feed off one another. Christians who wish to take effective action can use both channels in the service of justice.

WORKBENCH

Making your first speech

At some point you may have to make a short speech to the general public. Here are some do's and don'ts

• *Work out beforehand the three exact points you wish people to go away with. If you have only five minutes or less you can effectively make only one point. Sum up each point in a memorable way, make it pithy and sharp. Don't be afraid of controversy if it is necessary.*

• *Illustrate each point with a story from the locality. Make sure the story is accurate if it is a true story. If it is a fictional story make sure it will hold people's interest. If you use a funny story make sure that it is relevant.*

• *If you use statistics use no more than you need. One or two are usually sufficient. Give them life.*

• *If you are critical of another position make sure you are fair. Leave people with your positive alternative.*

• *Try and imagine the kind of questions people*

have in their mind about the issue. Try and speak to those questions rather than imposing your own agenda.

- Tell them what you're going to say, say it, and then tell them what you've said. Drive the point home. Use a different way of expressing yourself when you summarize your main point. Make it catchy. Don't use a sermon voice. Keep it light. Always keep exactly to time. Never run over.
- Practice on a friendly but critical friend beforehand.
- Pick out somebody in the crowd and speak to them. This can avoid the nerves that come when faced with a crowd. If your friend has come pretend you are delivering it to him or her again.
- Don't apologize for yourself or for your speech.
- Do write the whole thing down but be sufficiently familiar with it that you are not reading.
- As you speak look from side to side of the room addressing the whole gathering. Project your voice to the back of the hall.
- Always pray beforehand.
- If you get hecklers carry on. Don't try to answer them. You're too inexperienced. Remember they are trying to put you off. Don't let them.
- If you are depressed when you finish speaking, take no notice of yourself.
- Don't go looking for praise afterwards, you might get a rude shock.
- Whatever happens put it behind you, learn from your experience and determine to be even better next time. If it goes well give thanks to God. Never rest on your laurels (whatever they are!).
- Remember the two golden rules:
    1. All good speakers are disciplined speakers.
    2. It's not what you say that matters, it's what they hear.

"Make sure it will hold people's interest."

"If you get hecklers carry on."

'*On pre-sent trends one fifth of all arable land will be lost by AD 2,000; one third of tropical forests will be destroyed; and the world's deserts will have been increased by two thirds.*'
Maurice Sinclair

'*We have not been put on this planet to destroy it.*'
Prince Charles

THE GLOBAL SCENE

'How dare we teach our children about justice and humanity without doing anything at all for all those 82,000 children who are starving to death every day.' **Erik Dammann**

Throughout the 1980s we became increasingly aware that we live on a planet with finite resources. Its means of nurturing us, which have lasted for so long, are now beginning to fail and we have no-one to blame but ourselves. If we do not change our lifestyle and act swiftly to protect what is left we may not have long to live.

*t*his is our world

Every few years floods come to Bangladesh, one of the poorest countries in the world. Timber merchants and farmers are clearing forests in the Himalayan mountains especially in Nepal. With no trees to soak up the monsoon water it floods the Ganges and the Brahmaputra rivers. Similar patterns are emerging in the Andes and the Alps.

The problem is that natural disaster discriminates between rich and poor people. Who lives in the lowland delta in Bangladesh which is vulnerable? The poor, in their poorly built shanty towns.

Japan is also prone to earthquakes and typhoons. But because of good construction her 43 disasters from 1960-1981 average at only 63 deaths per disaster. Bangladesh had 63 disasters over the same period with an average death toll of over 10,000.

In 1972 an earthquake killed 5,000 in Managua, Nicaragua. A stronger quake in densely populated San Francisco in the previous year killed 65 people.

Back to Bangladesh. Over 100 million people live on that river delta. Over 15 million of them live less than 10 feet above sea level.

"...natural disaster discriminates between rich and poor people."

*g*lobal warming

By the time my children reach middle age 'global warming' (the trapping of the sun's rays beneath a cloud of pollution) means that the world's temperature will have risen by between 1.5 and 4.5 degrees. This is enough to make the oceans rise by 1.4 metres. It would make the Thames barrier obsolete and make British agriculture obsolete, as we now know it. Whole areas of the world would be under water.

"...the oceans will rise by 1.4 metres."

Ecological disaster may well replace nuclear disaster as the biggest threat to our planet. It will be an inheritance from us to our children. Acts of God turn out to be acts of men and women.

To the destruction of the rain forests (which is changing meteorological patterns) we can add the problem of acid rain; the problem of nuclear waste disposal; the pollution of our seas and rivers; the destruction of thousands of species of plants; the threat of the destruction of animals like whales; the destruction of the ozone layer; the increased hold which deserts have on our planet; the population explosion ... and you might be forgiven for thinking that I am deliberately drawing an apocalyptic vision which owes more to science fiction than scientific fact.

"We have borrowed the future from our children..."

Yet it remains true that all these things are due, in part, to our age of consumption – we have raped the world of its resources in the name of growth and have seen the world as ours. We have borrowed the future from our children and we cannot pay it back.

It is because of this that so many people are getting involved in Green issues. Groups like Greenpeace, Friends of the Earth, ARK, and the Christian Ecology Group have been trying to convince us for some time that we all have a duty to get involved. Each of these organizations will respond to an approach from an individual who wishes to get involved.

Many people find that the Green Agenda gives them a whole approach to living as a human being. Many Christians are now asking why the Christian church has not given such teaching before. The fact is that all is not lost. If we all act now we may still be in time.

*W*hat can we do?

It is in this area that we are most subject to

paralysis. We cannot conceive that anything we might do will have any effect on the planet as a whole. But there is a principle which is applied to peacemaking with people which can be applied to being at peace with the planet. *Be careful to do what is right in the eyes of everybody. If it is possible, as far as it depends on you, live at peace with everyone.*

"...all is not lost."

(Romans 12:17b-18)

Firstly, the context for our actions is not what effect they will have, but our duty before God to do what is right. It may well be that our actions have little outcome but that does not mean that we are to live without integrity before God and others. Secondly, notice the words 'as far as it depends on you' we are to live at peace with all people and to do that we must be responsible for those things which are in our power. Responsible stewardship of God's world is part of Christian peacemaking.

"Responsible stewardship of God's world..."

Peacemaking is not just about the absence of aggression but about the creation of something the Bible calls *shalom*. This is not just peace but wholeness, with justice and human rights. If we live in such a way that there is not enough for others then how can we be said to be 'at peace with everybody'.

(2 Corinthians 13:11)

Three issues arise out of this discussion.

1. How can we live appropriately in the light of the crisis, which is now looming on the horizon, in the management of our planet?

2. How can we provide long term development for those who are hardest hit by the problems? How can this be done in such a way as will not exacerbate the problems they already have?

3. How can we respond most effectively as individuals to the recurrent emergency appeals which are going to become more familiar as the world's eco-systems are increasingly disrupted?

Some practical ideas for us as individuals are given in the workbench at the end of this chapter. But the Green Agenda and the response of our country to Third World issues will always be a key area for lobbying Parliament and for those involved in educational work.

Perhaps the wisest words in this whole nightmare about environmental breakdown were spoken by marine biologist, Kenneth Kamlet, when he said, 'If it turns out that we are being more protective than necessary, posterity will forgive us.'

As far as it is in our power, let's live at peace with God's world.

Supporting development agencies

Some development agencies look at the problems which cause poverty. Many of them have educational departments with materials for children of all ages which could be used in a school or in a holiday club for local children. Others will send a speaker if you are willing to fund the trip.

Yet there are many other things you can do in this area. Some agencies will link you with a particular family or child who will correspond with you and with whom you develop a relationship. Still others will link your church with a church in the Third World in a relationship which might have far reaching consequences for both churches.

The possibilities are enormous. Why not write to these agencies and see the kind of work they are doing and the facilities they are offering. You may be surprised by the range of work being done by Traidcraft Exchange for instance. After all, how out of date is your knowledge of what these agencies are doing?

Serving abroad

I mentioned above that you might like to con-

"...let's live at peace with God's world."

sider going abroad for a period in order to be of service to others. It will not only be a service to them but you will learn a great deal yourself. There are lessons about one's own culture which can only be learned by stepping outside it. If you are frightened of settling down into a materialistic routine like many others around you, then going to the Third World while you are young will leave an indelible impression on you and make conformity to society that much harder.

There are many ways of doing this, either with an organization like VSO (Voluntary Service Overseas) or a Christian organization such as Christians Abroad or Interserve. Other organizations are listed at the end of Kathy Keay's *How to make the world less hungry*.

"The possibilities are enormous."

Frameworks, 1990

*E*urope

The British and Irish must not forget that we are part of Europe. After 1992 many trade barriers will have come down. The movement of people and money will be much more evident. Are those living in Europe going to grasp the positive opportunities this will provide? In recent years the British seem to have been the most reluctant Europeans, regarding it as a threat to our national identity. Surely as Christians we should see its potential and embrace it.

This is a good time to learn another language and to go and learn from other cultures and serve other people in their own country.
• If we pray for 'those in authority' we should pray for those MEPs in Brussels.
• 60% of our legislation currently is initiated in Brussels. Are we beginning to lobby Brussels?
• All that has been said about developing a relationship with our MP also applies to our MEPs.
• Students, in particular, will be able to take courses in different European universities. This

would extend fellowship between Christians and strengthen the ties between Christian groups.

WORKBENCH

Green practice

Here's a checklist which gives practical suggestions as to how we can live with integrity in the light of these issues.

- *Recycling waste, using bottle banks, shopping for environmentally-friendly products. Eating healthily, eating less.*
- *Conservation action. Supporting a group which is dedicated to the preservation of wildlife, forests, flowers and endangered species.*
- *Campaigning for government policy which stops environmental pollution.*
- *Joining a local environmental group which monitors pollution control in your area.*
- *Ensuring that there is teaching on such issues in the local church.*
- *Supporting financially one of the development agencies such as Tear fund, Traidcraft, Christian Aid or Oxfam. Becoming an agent for Third World craft products.*
- *Ensuring that your church devotes time to development issues as well as a proportion of its budget.*
- *Prayerfully considering the possibility that you might be called to the Third World yourself.*
- *Setting up a convenant to an organization such as the Charities Aid Foundation so that you always have some money to hand (independent of your own financial state!) to give to disaster relief or long term development projects.*
- *Writing to the managers of your local supermarkets and stores about stocking environmentally sensitive products. Get others in your church/ neighbourhood to do the same.*
- *Finding out what resources do not exist in your*

"Eating healthily, eating less."

area and setting something up. Does anybody collect paper in your area for recycling? Sometimes this has been discontinued because it is said to be 'uneconomic'. Could you do it? Look into it.

You could think of more. Indeed it makes a good exercise in a group to sit down with some of the literature from the 'green' organizations and the development agencies and list as many practical ways of responding to these dilemmas as you can think of. It is amazing how much you can actually do. It turns out that the area in which you felt most paralysed may be the area where you feel the impact of living appropriately most personally.

One great resource in this area is The Green Consumer Guide *which will give you lots of ideas especially related to what you buy.*

"Could you do it? Look into it."

all that we have said in this book is geared to making a Christian impact in a hostile world. Our desire is to make our

world more pleasing to God. Whatever we do, we do for him.

Whether we work within specifically Christian structures and organizations, or opt to work with others

MAKING A CHRISTIAN IMPACT

who are committed to broadly similar goals as ourselves, we do everything as Christians. What does that mean? What is our strategy? I believe that out of our discussion seven things emerge that we should aim to become.

1. Perceptive. We need to learn to listen to the world. For a long time we were alienated from it and hid in our churches. Now we are learning to participate in society and to get involved. Soon we must learn to *anticipate* the changes in our society otherwise we will be too late with our response. *In the modern world Christians must anticipate in order to participate.* To do that we will need to become sensitive and perceptive as to the key areas of need in the world.

(Matthew 10:16)

2. Persuasive. We must learn to be articulate about *why* we believe what we believe. Christians are good at adopting slogans but often are not so good at giving reasons as to why these slogans are true. It is important that we study, discuss and debate. Never downgrade words. God has given us words to change the hearts and minds of people. We can no longer assume, in our multi-cultured society, that we have a right to be heard as Christians. We must win people by the power of our arguments and by the powerful witness of our lives.

"What is our strategy?"

3. Pastoral. We must always remain people-centred rather than system- or ideology-centred. If we are focused on God himself then our greatest desire will be for people who are all made in his image. All our thinking, whether it is about politics or the environment or anything else, must seek to serve the best interests of individuals and humanity as a whole. Also we must never downgrade the simple act of charity. We must never fly so high in our illusions about political action that we make the person who visits the elderly or has befriended a disabled person feel that her service is second rate. Pastoral care is also care of our world in the service of people.

"We must win people..."

4. Prayerful. If we neglect prayer as we take action we give the game away. We show that we think what we are doing is merely human and that we are the best judge of its consequences. But all we do in obedience to God, we do in co-operation with God. No person who loves God will want to leave him out of anything they do. Prayer changes the world and no social action will stand the test of eternity unless it is first soaked in prayer and carried out in the power of the Spirit. If God does not go with us in what we do how will we be distinctive?

(See 1 Thessalonians 5:17)

5. Prophetic. We live in a world in which the voice of the prophetic cannot be heard because we are too committed to the mediocre. Today, the job of the prophet, which is to challenge society and call God's people to new heights in their obedience, is doubly unwelcome, given the comfort which this world offers to the Christians who will not ask too many questions. If the church does not recover its obedience it will continue to be an unremarkable institution rather than the voice of God in a world which is deaf to truth.

6. Pragmatic. We must not fear being practical. If we only deal in words we shall be rightly condemned. All over the world Christians should be setting up small schemes which show the difference which the kingdom of God makes when its values are enshrined in people's lives. We may call governments to great acts but we are called also to put our message into practice. Whether it is hospice care, sheltered workshops, housing associations, employment projects, health care in the Third World, mother and toddlers groups, English lessons for Bengali women, a warm hand holding a lonely old lady's hand and a listening ear for her stories of days long gone, or a home for those who have never known family life, we must show that faith produces works which demonstrate the character of the one we have faith in.

"Prayer changes the world..."

7. *Political*. We must not be afraid of the political. The church must never be prejudiced in party politics. It stands over all parties and criticizes the provisionality of all programmes in the light of the kingdom of God. It also affirms that which is good across the party political divide. But if we are concerned about the whole person we must not be afraid about using political tools to bring about change in our world, so long as it is change for the good.

"We must not be afraid about using political tools..."

The writer of Ecclesiastes advises us, '*Whatever your hand finds to do, do it with all you might for in the grave, where you are going, there is neither working nor planning nor knowledge nor wisdom*'.

(Ecclesiastes 9:10)

You have one life to live for Christ. It is very short. In that time you can accomplish a great deal. Your life can make a difference. When we are dead and gone many may give thanks to God for our lives because of the way in which we were prepared to take a risk on their behalf.

You *can* change the world. Remember, one person plus God is a majority!

WORKBENCH

The user-friendly guide to taking action

This is a brief guide to some of the organizations and resources which are available to people wishing to do something. We have been very aware of the limitations of space and of the fact that, while compiling it, we have only scratched the surface of the available resources.

1. General Resources

The UK Christian Handbook *(Marc Europe/Evangelical Alliance/Bible Society, ed. Peter Brierly). An exhaustive annual directory of Christian organizations and resources. Costs around £15, but try your church or local library.*

2. General Help

The following organizations can help with a wide number of queries and put you in touch with the relevant Christian organization.

AFES *(Australian Federation of Evangelical Students), 16, Mill Hill Road, Bondi Junction, New South Wales, 2022 Australia.*

Christian Impact, *St Peters Church, Vere Street, London W1M 9HP, Tel: (01) 629 3615, or 79, Maid Marian Way, Nottingham, NG1 6AE, Tel: (0602) 585 731.*

CARE *(Christian Action Research and Education), 53, Romney Street, London SW1P 3RF, Tel: (01) 233 0455. (Same number for* **Care Trust** *and* **Care Campaigns**.)

The Jubilee Centre, *Jubilee House, 3, Hooper Street, Cambridge CB1 2NZ, Tel: (0223) 311 596. (Number also covers* **Familybase** *and the* **Keep Sunday Special Campaign**.)

Kingdom Trust, *31, Lady Bay Road, Nottingham NG2 5BJ, Tel: (0602) 455 542.*

Evangelical Alliance, *186, Kennington Park Road,*

London SE11 4BT, Tel: (01) 582 0228.

ZADOK Institute for Christianity and Society, *Blackall Street, Barton, ACT, 2600 Australia, Tel: (062) 73 1634.*

Evangelicals for Social Action, *5107, Newhall Street, Philadelphia, Pa 19144 USA, Tel: (215) 438 1670.*

3. Life Issues

The Society for the Protection of the Unborn Child, *7, Tufton Street, London SW1P 3QN, Tel: (01) 222 5845.*

LIFE, *118-120, Warwick Street, Leamington Spa, Warwickshire, Tel: (0926) 21587.*
See also under **CARE** *(Section 2).*

4. AIDS

London Lighthouse, *178, Lancaster Road, London W11 1QU, Tel: (01) 727 2018.*

ACET *(AIDS Care Education and Training), PO Box 1323, London W5 5TF, Tel: (01) 840 7879*

Mildmay Mission Hospital, *Hackney Road, London E2 7NA, Tel: (01) 739 2331.*

5. Broadcasting

If you have a comment or complaint contact:

Independent Broadcasting Authority *(IBA), 70, Brompton Road, London SW3 1EY (TV or advertising).*

BBC, *Broadcasting House, Portland Place, London 1A 1AA, Tel: (01) 580 4468.*

Broadcasting Standards Council, *5-8, The Sanctuary, London SW1P 3JS, Tel: (01) 233 0544.*

National Viewers and Listeners Association *(NVALA), Blahernae, Ardleigh, Colchester CO7 7RH, Tel: (0206) 230 123.*

6. Green Issues

The Green Party, *10, Station Parade, Balham High Road, London SW12 9AZ, Tel: (01) 673 0045.*

Friends of the Earth, *26-28, Underwood Street, London N1 7JQ, Tel: (01) 490 1555.*

Greenpeace, *30-31, Islington Green, London N1 8XE, Tel: (01) 354 5100.*

ARK, *The Ark Trust, 498-500, Harrow Road, London W9 3QA, Tel: (01) 968 6780.*

7. Housing and Homelessness

CHAR, *5-15, Cromer Street, London WC1H 8LS, Tel: (01) 833 2071.*

Shelter, *88, Old Street, London EC1V 9HU, Tel: (01) 253 0202.*

CARE Homes Programme, c/o Steve McQuoid, Director of **Caring Initiatives**, *53, Romney Street, London SW1P 3RF, Tel: (01) 233 0455. (This address is a general contact for the CARE homes register.)*

National Federation of Housing Co-operatives, *88, Old Street, London EC1V 9AX, Tel: (01) 608 2494.*

National Federation of Housing Associations, *175, Grays Inn Road, London WC1H 8LR, Tel: (01) 833 2071.*

The Simon Community, *St Joseph's House, 129, Malden Road, London NW5 4HS, Tel: (01) 485 6639.*

8. Prisons and Rehabilitation

Prison Fellowship, *Moulsham Mill, Parkway, Chelmsford, Essex CM2 7PX, Tel: (0245) 490 249.*

NACRO *(National Association for the Care and Resettlement of Offenders) 169, Clapham Road, London SW9 0PU, Tel: (01) 278 9815.*

National Association of Victim Support Schemes, *17a, Electric Lane, Brixton, London SW9 8LA, Tel: (01) 737 2010.*

9. Education

Education Group *(AFES), 16, Mill Hill Road, Bondi Junction, New South Wales, 2022 Australia.*

Council on Christian Education in Schools, *100, Flinders Street, Melbourne 3000, Australia.*

Christians in Education, *PO Box 214, St Albans, Herts AL4 OLE, Tel: (0702) 78485.*

Stapleford House, *Wesley Place, Stapleford, Nottingham NG9 8DP, Tel: (0602) 396270.*

Association of Christian Teachers, *2, Romeland Hill, St Albans, Herts AL3 4ET, Tel: (0727) 40298.*

Scripture Union in Schools, *130, City Road, London EC1V 2NJ, Tel: (01) 782 0013.*

10. Childcare

Child Poverty Action Group, *4th Floor, 1-5 Bath Street, London EC1V 9PY, Tel: (01) 253 3406.*

National Foster Care Association, *Francis House, Francis Street, London SW1P 1DE, Tel: (01) 828 6266.*

National Children's Home, *85, Highbury Park, London N5 1UD, Tel: (01) 266 2033.*

The Children's Society, *Edward Rudolf House, Margery Street, London WC1X OJL.*

National Society for the Prevention of Cruelty to Children, *67, Saffron Hill, London EC1N 8RS, Tel: (01) 242 1626.*

11. Disability

PHAB, *Tavistock House North, Tavistock Square, London WC1H 9HX, Tel: (01) 388 1963.*

Disabled Christian Fellowship, *50, Clare Road, Kingswood, Bristol, Avon BS15 1PJ, Tel: (0272) 616 141.*

Mental Health Foundation, *8, Hallam Street, London W1N 6DH.*

MENCAP, *123, Golden Lane, London EC1Y ORT, Tel: (01) 253 9433.*

12. The Elderly

Help the Aged, *St James Walk, London EC1R OBE, Tel: (01) 253 0253.*

Age Concern, *60, Pitcairn Road, Mitcham, Surrey CR4 3LL, Tel: (01) 640 5431.*

13. Houses of Parliament

House of Commons, *Westminster, London SW1A OAA, Tel: (01) 219 3000.*

House of Lords, *Westminster, London SW1A OYW, Tel: (01) 219 3107.*

14. European Parliament

European Parliament Information Office, *2, Queen Anne's Gate, London SW1H 9AA, Tel: (01) 222 0411.*

15. Human Rights

Amnesty International, *5 Roberts Place, off Bowling Green Lane, London EC1R OEJ, Tel: (01) 251 8371.*

Jubilee Campaigns, *PO Box 80, Cobham, Surrey KT11 2BQ, Tel: (0932) 67037.*

National Council for Civil Liberties, *21 Tabard Street, London SE1 4LA.*

16. Race Issues

Evangelical Christians for Racial Justice, *12, Bell Barn Shopping Centre, Cregoe Street, Birmingham B15 2DZ, Tel: (021) 622 5799.*

British Council of Churches Community and Race Relations Unit, *2, Eaton Gate, London SW1W 9BL.*

Commission for Racial Equality, *Elliott House, 10-12, Allington Street, London SW1E 5EH.*

Runnymede Trust, *37a, Grays Inn Road, London WC1X 8PP.*

The Centre for Black and White Christian Partnership, *Selly Oak Colleges, Central House, Birmingham B29 6LE.*

West Indian Evangelical Alliance, *71, Hayter Road, Brixton, London SW2 5AD.*

17. Development Agencies

Christian Aid, *PO Box 100, London SE1 7RT, Tel: (01) 620 4444 (same address and telephone number for 'One World Week').*

Tear Fund, *100, Church Road, Teddington, Middx. TW11 8QE, Tel: (01) 977 9144.*

Traidcraft plc *and* **Traidcraft Exchange** *(the charity), Kingsway, Gateshead NE11 ONE, Tel: (091) 491 0591.*

World Development Movement, *Bedford Chambers, Covent Garden, London WC2E 8HA, Tel: (01) 836 3672.*

18. Trade Unions

Industrial Christian Fellowship, *St Katherine Kree Church, 86, Leadenhall Street, London EC3A 3DH.*

Workers Educational Association, *8, Upper Berkeley Street, London W1H 8BY.*

19. Urban Issues

Evangelical Coalition for Urban Mission, *Lawrence Hall, Poplar, London E1, Tel: (01) 476 3651.*

Shaftesbury Society, *Shaftesbury House, 2a, Amity Grove, Raynes Park, London SW20 OLH, Tel: (01) 946 6634.*

Frontier Youth Trust, *130, City Road, London EC1, Tel: (01) 511 1296.*

See also **EUTP** *(Evangelical Urban Training Project) under 'Housing'.*

20. Reconciliation Groups

Christian CND, *22, Underwood Street, London N1 7JG, Tel: (01) 250 4010.*

Evangelical Peacemakers, *59, Harold Street, Hereford HR1 2QU, Tel: (0432) 55724.*

21. Voluntary Organizations

Careforce, *130, City Road, London EC1V 2NJ, Tel: (01) 250 1966.*

Christians Abroad, *1, Stockwell Green, London SW9 9HP, Tel: (01) 737 7811.*

NCVO, *National Council for Voluntary Organizations, 26, Bedford Square, London WC1B 3HW, Tel: (01) 636 4066.*

The National Association of Citizen's Advice Bureaux, *Myddleton House, 115-123, Pentonville Road, London N1 9LZ, Tel: (01) 833 2181.*

Voluntary Service Overseas, *9, Belgrave Square, London SW1X 8PW, Tel: (01) 235 5191.*

22. Giving

Charities Aid Foundation, *48, Pembury Road, Tonbridge, Kent TN9 2JD, Tel: (0732) 771 333.*

23. Debt

Money Advice Association, *20, Grosvenor Gardens, London SW1W ODH, Tel: (01) 730 3469.*

See also **NACAB** *above.*

Familybase, *see Jubilee House above.*

24. Written Resources

F. Beckett, Called to Action (Fount, 1989).

A. Dubs, Lobbying: An Insider's Guide to the Parliamentary Process *(Pluto Press).*

MAKING AN IMPACT

Martyn Eden and Ernest Lucas, Being Transformed (*Marshalls, 1988*).

John Elkington and Julia Hailes, The Green Consumer Guide (*Gollancz, 1988*).

Charles Elliot, Signs of Our Times: Prayer and Action to Change the World (*Marshalls, 1988*).

Ian Greer, Right to be Heard (*IGA, 1975*).

Journal of Christian Education (Australia), *available from AFES (see section 9)*.

Patrick Logan, A Life to be Lived: homelessness and pastoral care (*DLT, 1989*).

Charles Martin, Schools Now: A Parent's Guide (*Lion, 1988*).

John Stott, Issues Facing Christians Today (*Marshalls, 1984*).

Third Way magazine, *2, Chester House, Pages Lane, Muswell Hill, London N10 1PR, Tel: (01) 883 0372*.

Zadok Perspectives (*published by the Zadok Institute for Christianity and Society, Australia. See section 2*).